Early Television

Name ______________________

Read the story.

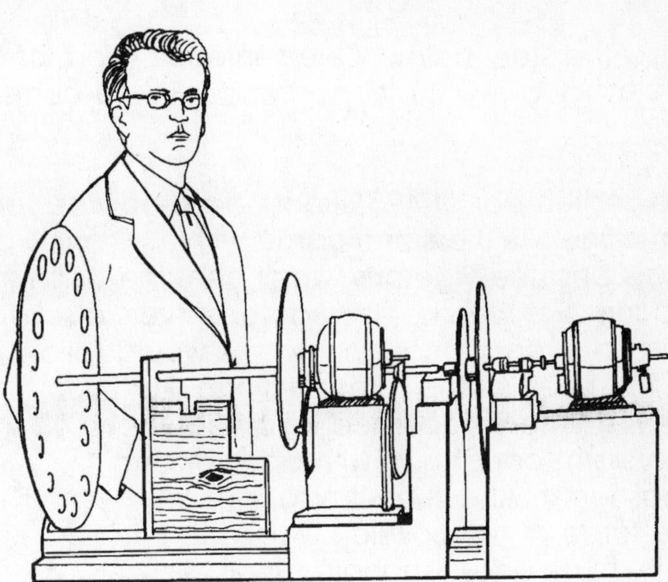

John Baird grew up in Scotland before World War I. As a boy, he liked to make electrical things. Although the telephone was already invented in 1876 before he was born, he made his own phone and hooked it up to the homes of his four best friends who lived on his street. No one objected to the wires going in and out of windows along the street until after a wind knocked a wire down during a storm one night. A man driving his horse-drawn wagon did not see the downed wire in the dark, and he was pulled from his wagon by it. He was furious and demanded that all the wires be taken down.

John continued to experiment and build electrical things. When he was at the university studying engineering, the radio was invented. He realized that someday pictures would be sent over distances just as sounds were starting to be sent.

He became ill and was unable to work at a job. The doctor ordered him to go to the seaside and rest. He lived in a small room and had very little money, but he spent all that he could afford on old radio parts and other electrical items. He laid wires out all over his room. He experimented sending a picture from one room to another and made a working television set in 1926. Many men worked to develop television, but what set John apart from the others was he did it alone and for very little money.

Number the sentences below in order to tell about one of the people who helped develop the television. Not all of the sentences will be used.

____ One night there was a huge storm.

____ John Baird was born in Scotland.

____ Baird fought in World War I.

____ Baird made his own telephone.

____ John Baird produced a working television set.

____ He realized when he was in college that someday there would be television.

____ The telephone was invented.

____ He fixed the fallen wire and continued to use the telephones with his friends.

____ Five friends talked to one another on a homemade telephone.

____ John Baird was in poor health and could not hold a job.

- Circle the highest temperature.

150°F **100°C** **200°F**

Bermuda's Savior

Name ______________________________

Read the story below. One sentence is out of order. Circle it and rewrite the sentences in the correct order.

In September of 1951 Bermuda prepared for a powerful hurricane. As the storm came within 10 miles of the island's coast and the vigorous winds bent the palm trees to the ground, the weather bureau observers discovered that an even stronger hurricane would follow on the heels of the present storm. For the first time in recorded weather history, one storm caught up with another and smashed it. And then it happened. The force of the collision weakened both hurricanes, changing their courses. Both storms turned away from the island. They blew out to sea where they wasted their energy on an empty ocean, and Bermuda was spared.

• Circle the longest month.

February March April

Forgotten Cities

Name ______________________________

The sentences in the story are out of order. One sentence does not belong. Cross this sentence out and rewrite the story so the sentences are in order.

They are simply places left empty by their former inhabitants. During the 1800's, mining areas sprang up all over America with the discovery of gold and silver. There are no ghosts in ghost towns. Hay was grown by the farmers. There are many such ghost towns in the western United States. When the mines ran dry or it was no longer profitable to mine them the treasure seekers left and the towns died. New towns popped up overnight as hotels, saloons and small businesses opened to serve the new population. Prospectors rushed to each discovery to dig or pan for the precious metals.

____

____

____

____

____

____

____

____

____

____

____

____

- Circle the longest time period.

a leap year **6 months** **a regular year**

The Unsinkable Ship

Name ______________________________

The sentences in the story are out of order. One sentence does not belong. Cross this sentence out and rewrite the story so the rest of the sentences are in order.

German engineers raised her and began repairs. The Germans raised the ship once more and repaired it. The British liner, the Titanic, hit an iceberg in the Atlantic Ocean and sank on its maiden voyage. Before the Dutch liner, the Westerdam, ever made her first journey, she had been sunk three times. After the war the Dutch raised the Westerdam and rebuilt it as a passenger ship. Construction had begun on her in 1939, but when the Germans invaded the Netherlands the following year, they seized her and took over her construction. Dutch patriots sneaked on board during repairs. In 1942 an Allied bomb hit the Westerdam, and she went to the bottom of the sea. This time Dutch patriots attached explosives to the hull and sank the ship for the third time. They opened valves in the hull of the ship to let in water. The Westerdam went down again.

- Circle the largest vessel.

canoe **steamboat** **tugboat**

Skill: Reading a Map

Air Routes of the United States

Name ______________________

Look at the map. List the states over which each route passes. Specific directions are given below for each route.

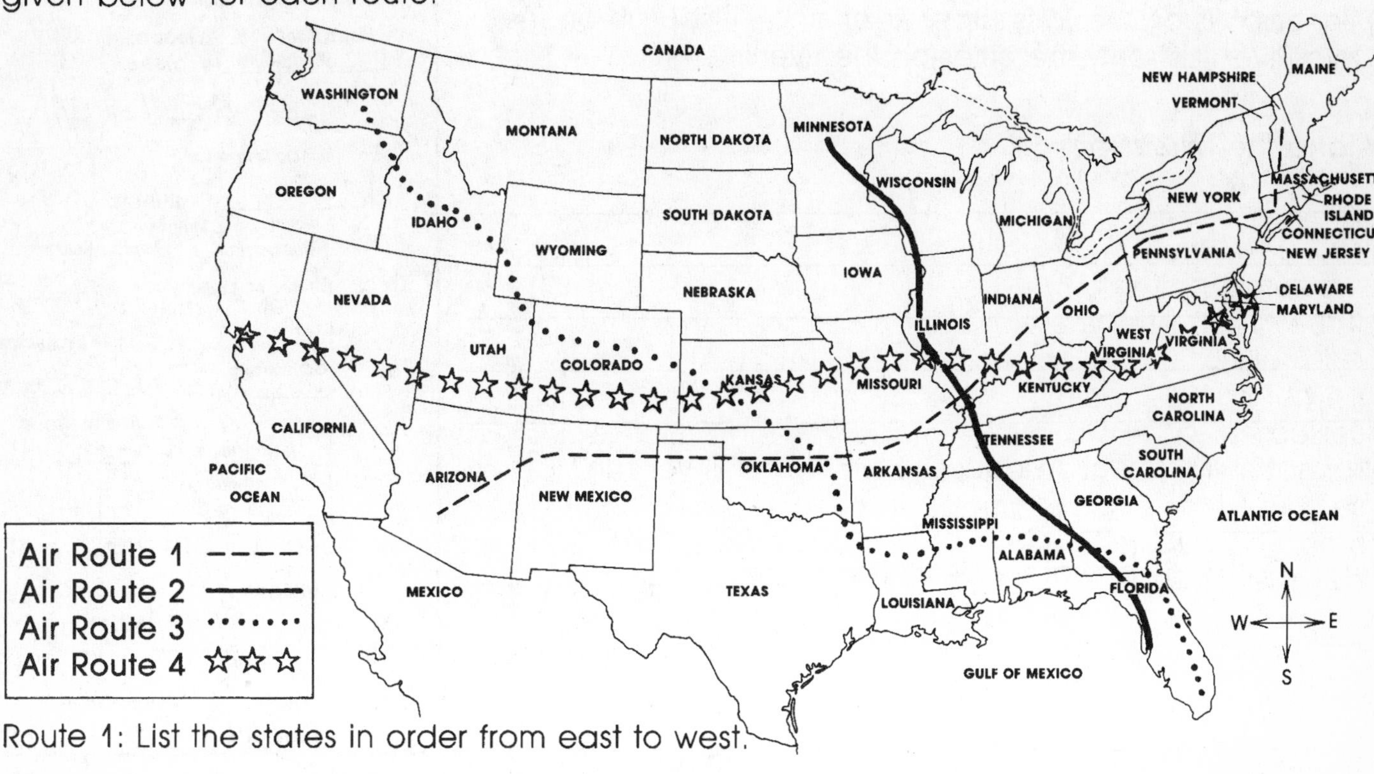

Route 1: List the states in order from east to west.

____

____

____

Route 2: List the states this route follows in order from south to north.

____

____

Route 3: List the states this route follows in order from the Northwest to the Southeast.

____

____

____

Route 4: List the states in order from the West Coast to the East Coast.

____

____

____

- Circle the lowest number.

99.01 **98.07** **98.5** **98.05**

Follow the Rivers

Name ______________________

Look at each river's path. List the cities and their states in the order each river flows through them. Start with Minneapolis on the Mississippi River and Pittsburgh on the Ohio River. List only the cities on the rivers.

Mississippi River

Minneapolis
St. Paul
Minnesota
Wisconsin
Fairmount
LaCrosse
Iowa
Davenport
Illinois
Quincy
Springfield
Missouri
St. Louis
Jefferson City
Kentucky
Carthage
Columbus
Tennessee
Arkansas
Memphis
Helena
Mississippi River
Greenville
Louisiana
Mississippi
N
W E
S
New Orleans
Gulf of Mexico

Along the Mississippi

____

____

____

____

____

In what main direction does the Mississippi River run?

____

Into what body of water does it flow? ______________

Along the Ohio

____

____

____

____

____

____

____

____

____

____

In what two main directions does the Ohio River run? ______________

Into what body of water does it flow? ______________________

____

• Circle the largest number.

4 tens, 8 ones **6 sevens, 7 ones** **5 tens, 0 ones**

Traveling to a Destination

Name ______________________________

Look at each road map and list the cities in the order of each heading. List only the cities that are on the main route.

Kansas City to Denver

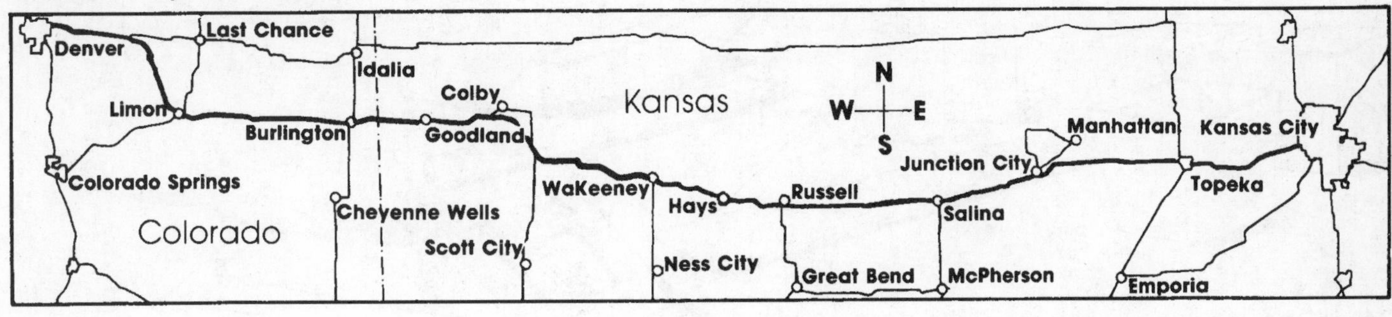

____

____

____

Salt Lake City to Cheyenne

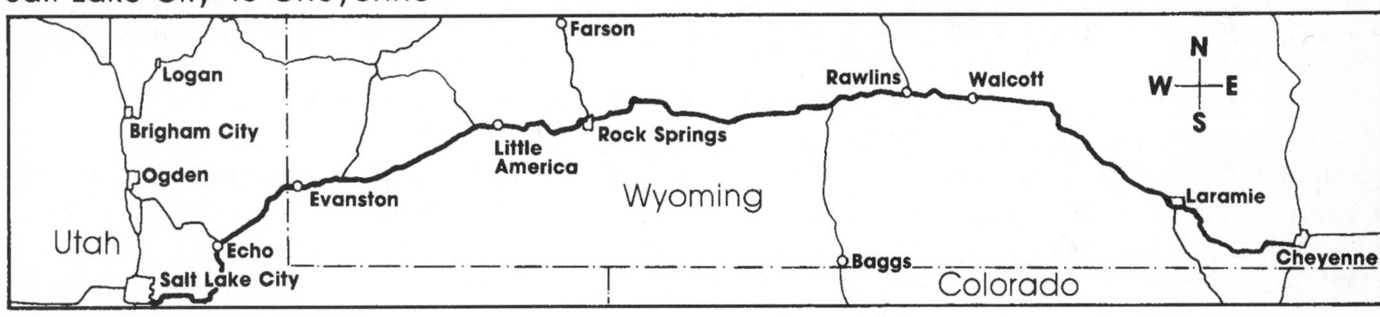

____

____

____

Little Rock to Texarkana

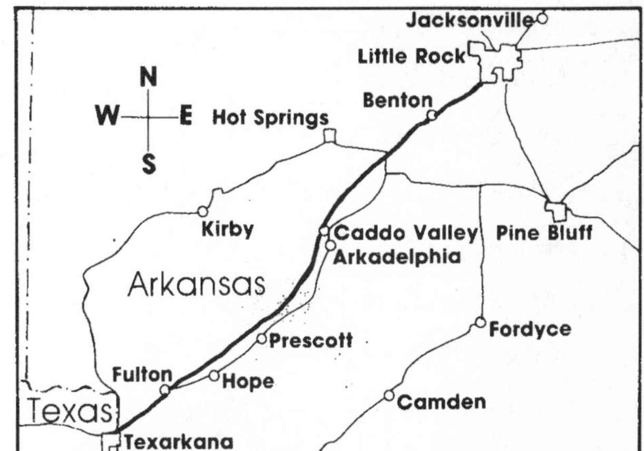

____

____

____

____

____

____

- Circle the warmest temperature.

32°F 32°C −5°C

Science Project

Name ______________________________

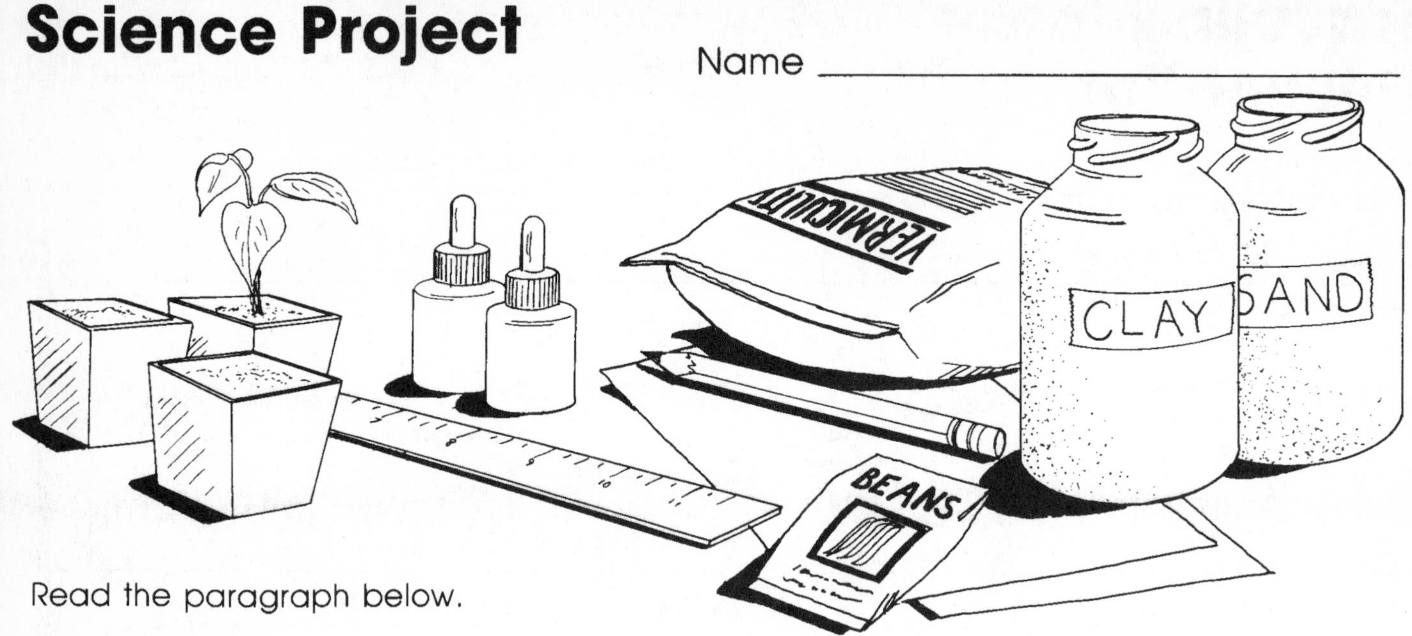

Read the paragraph below.

The first step in a science project is to have an idea. The idea may come from a personal interest or from something that has been studied. The next step is developing the idea. Background information may be gathered from science textbooks and/or reference books. Reading about the topic will help you decide how to set up a project. Gather together the necessary equipment and supplies that will be needed to prepare your project. Be sure not to use anything that may be harmful or be harmed. Keep accurate records to use when you write your report. The report should include what is expected to be learned, how the project will be carried out, what results will be obtained, and what conclusions should be reached. When the report is completed, the project is ready to be set up. In setting up an exhibit, arrange your project neatly. Make all labels legible. If your project includes a demonstration, test it to make certain it does what it is supposed to do. Repeat the test to see that the same conclusion is reached. Now you are ready to show your project.

Number the sentences to show how to do a science project.

____ Set up the project.

____ Write a report.

____ Get an idea for the project.

____ Perform the scientific demonstration, if you have one.

____ Develop the idea by doing research.

____ Keep records from which a report may be written.

____ Show off the project.

____ Repeat the demonstration.

• Circle the correct word choices to make the statement true.

At dusk the sun (sets, rises) and at dawn it (sets, rises).

Germination

Name ______________________________

Number the pictures of the developing plant in the correct order. Then use the pictures to rewrite the sentences following the order of the numbered pictures.

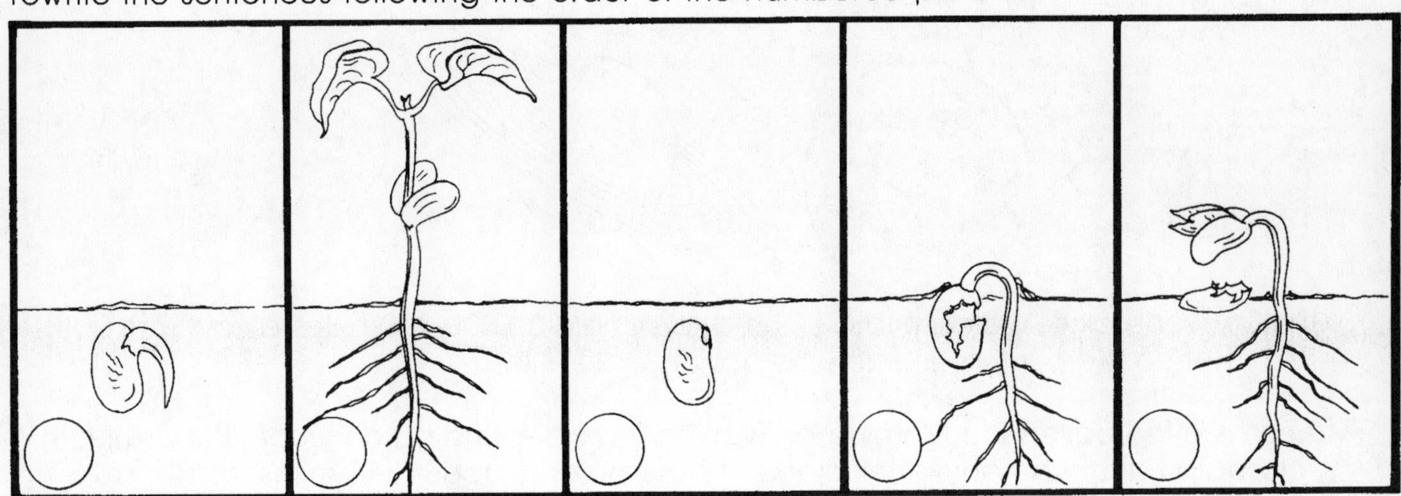

The seed splits and the hypocotyl extends downward to anchor the plant into the ground and become the primary root.
As the plant grows, it develops leaves above ground.
The seed covering falls off and the cotyledons split open and free the bud that produces the plant's first leaves.
A root system grows out from the primary root and the stem breaks through the soil.
A seed has all the parts it needs to form a new plant, but it is inactive before it starts to grow.

1. ______________________________

2. ______________________________

3. ______________________________

4. ______________________________

5. ______________________________

- Circle the correct word to make the statement true.

The (perimeter, circumference) is the distance around the outside of any shape.

Planets

Name ______________________________

Number the planets of our Solar System according to their size with 1 representing the smallest planet.

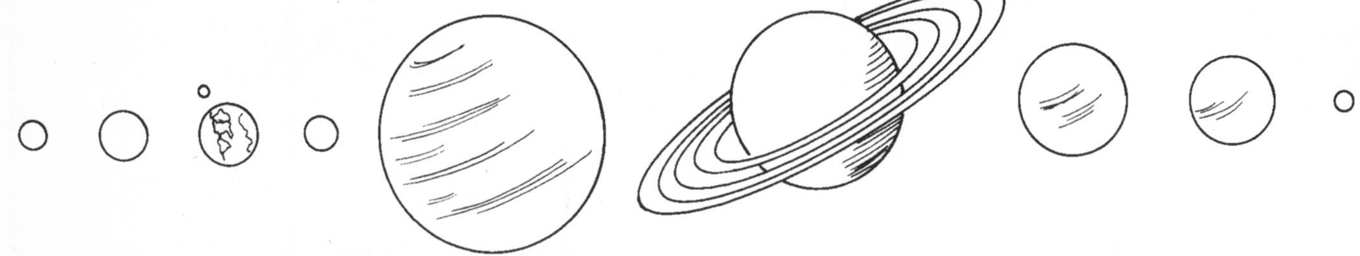

____ Mercury is the closest planet to the sun and still it is 36,000,000 miles away from it. It is very hot on Mercury. Its diameter is about 3,100 miles.

____ Venus is often called the Morning or Evening Star, depending on when it is visible. It is closer to Earth than any other planet. Its diameter is about 315 miles less than Earth's.

____ Life on Earth has made it possible to measure the planet accurately. Earth's diameter is 7,926 miles. It is surrounded by an atmosphere of gases that extends upward about 500 miles.

____ Mars appears to have some features that suggest there might be life on it. It's almost half the size of Earth — 4,140 miles across its center, but it takes Mars 687 Earth days to go around the sun because it is almost 50,000,000 miles further away from the sun than Earth.

____ Jupiter is the largest planet. It has 12 moons, four of which can be seen without a telescope even though Jupiter is at least 367,000,000 miles from Earth. One of its moons has a larger diameter than Mercury's.

____ Saturn is the most like Jupiter. It is closest to it in size. It is large enough to be seen by the naked eye, but its rings must be viewed with a telescope.

____ Uranus is the seventh planet from the sun. It was discovered in 1781 by accident. Sometimes it is called Neptune's twin, although it is over 2,000 miles wider.

____ Neptune was discovered in 1846. It may only be seen with a telescope although its diameter is 27,000 miles — almost three and a half times greater than Earth's.

____ Pluto is the newest planet; it was discovered in 1930. It is so far away that there are many unanswered questions about it, but it is estimated that its diameter is 3,600 miles.

- Circle the prefixes below that indicate sequence by position.

com- ante- fore- dis- pre- pro-

Make a Pop-Up Card

Name ____________________

Number the directions below each box to show how to make a pop-up card.

Draw a face, person, or anim al on a third piece of paper. Color it and fold it in half with the picture side out.

___

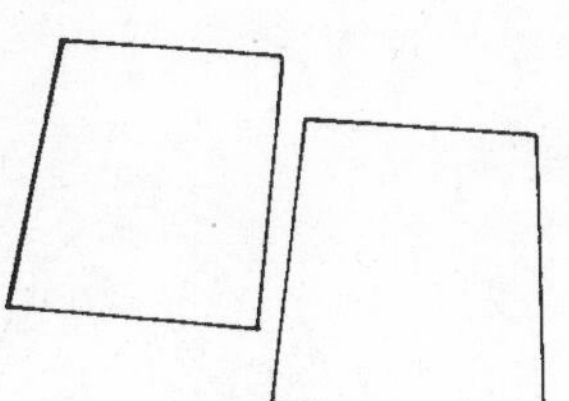

Select two pieces of paper the same size.

___

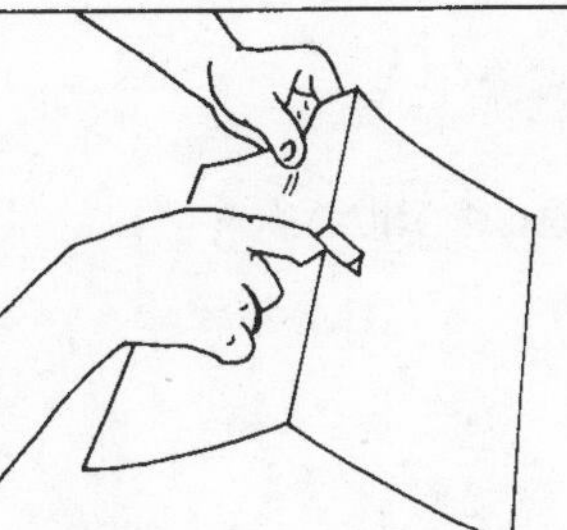

Open the paper and push the cut strip though to the other side.

___

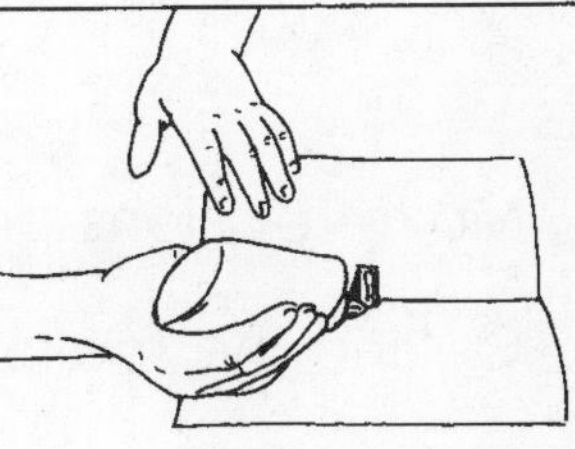

Apply glue on each side of the strip.

___

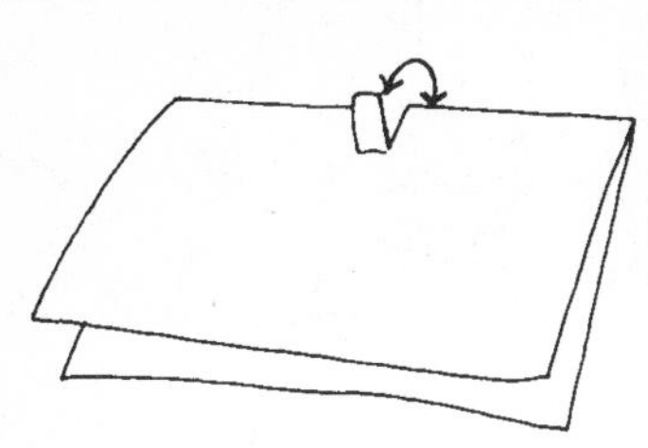

Fold the cut strip back and then fold it forward again.

___

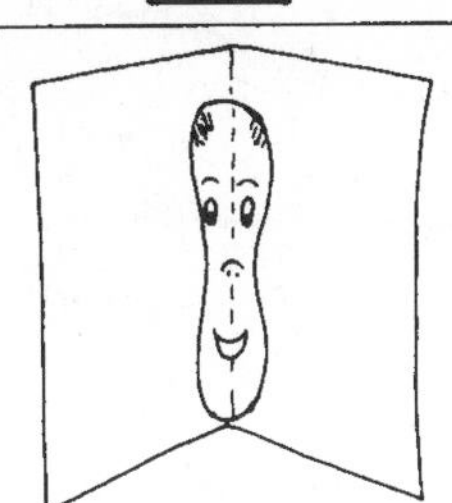

Put your folded figure on the strip with glue. Decorate the rest of the inside.

___

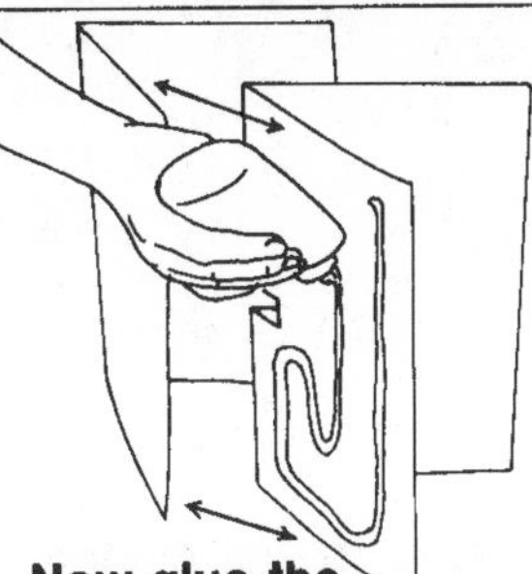

Now glue the two papers together. Decorate the outside.

___

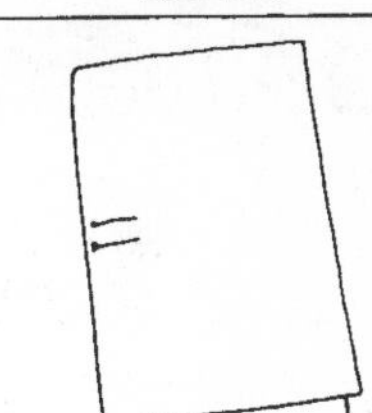

Start at the dots. Draw two parallel lines about 1 inch long toward the center of the front of the paper.

___

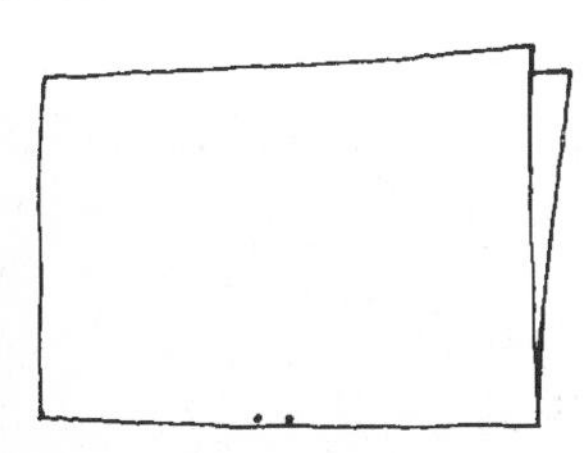

On one piece of paper, mark two dots about ½ inch apart in the middle of the folded edge.

___

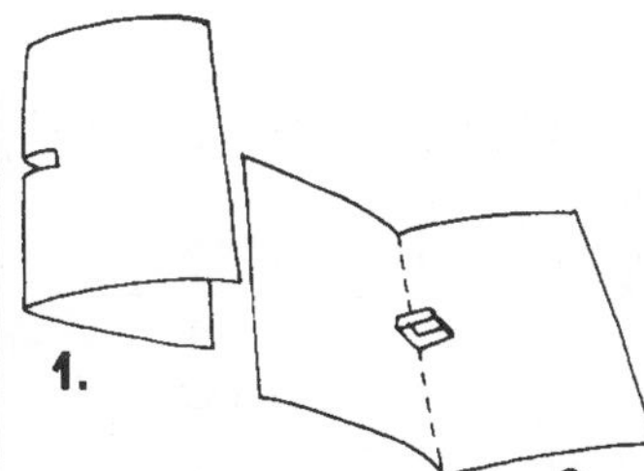

Close the card and press firmly. Then open to see the pop-up strip.

___

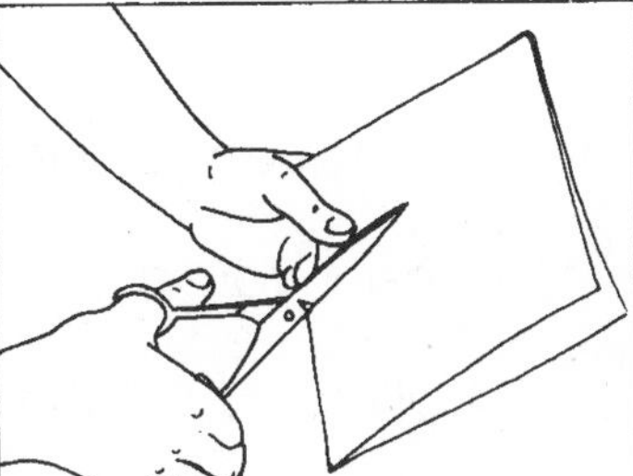

Cut on the lines starting from the folded edge.

___

Fold each paper in half and then put one piece to the side.

___

Now follow the directions. If you have them in the right order you will be able to make a pop-up card.

- Circle the correct word to make the statement true.

A team wins a World Series (before, after) it wins the pennant.

Do It in Order

Name ______________________________

Number the instructions in the correct order to show how a composition is written.

____ Make revisions and corrections.

____ Outline the main points.

____ Decide on a subject.

____ Write a first draft.

____ Rewrite it in its final form.

____ Examine what you have written.

____ List the details.

Number the instructions in the correct order for starting a business.

____ Figure out the amount of money that will be needed to get the business started.

____ Set any profit aside to put back into the business as necessary or to pay yourself a bonus.

____ Keep a record of the money earned and expenses incurred by the business.

____ Decide what type of business you are interested in.

____ Pay back the loan in installments and pay yourself a salary.

____ Get a loan.

____ Buy whatever equipment or materials you will need.

____ Solicit jobs or advertise your business.

____ Include your time, money paid out and continuing expenses when you figure what your monthly expenses might be.

- Circle the correct word to make the statement true.

  The (anterior, interior, posterior) part of the horse is the last thing seen jumping over the fence.

An Unusual Sweep

Name ____________________

Number the instructions in the correct order to show how to use a metal detector.

____ Thrust a sharp implement like a screwdriver straight down from where the sound is loudest.

____ Replace the soil and smooth it over so it looks the same as you found it.

____ Sweep the head of the detector slowly from one side to another, keeping the head as close to the ground as possible.

____ The first thing you must keep in mind when using a metal detector is that you have to have patience.

____ Poke around until the hard object is located.

____ Move ahead slowly so that each sweep overlaps the one before it.

____ Remove the object from the ground.

____ Once you have located the signal, move the head of the detector back and forth until the center of it is over the point at which the signal is loudest.

____ Remove as little of the soil as is necessary to reach the indicated object.

____ If you hear a beep, go back over the ground to locate the signal.

• Circle the correct word to make the statement true.

The moderator's (summation, introduction) that followed the evening's program clarified the speakers' remarks.

Finding a Job

Name ______________________

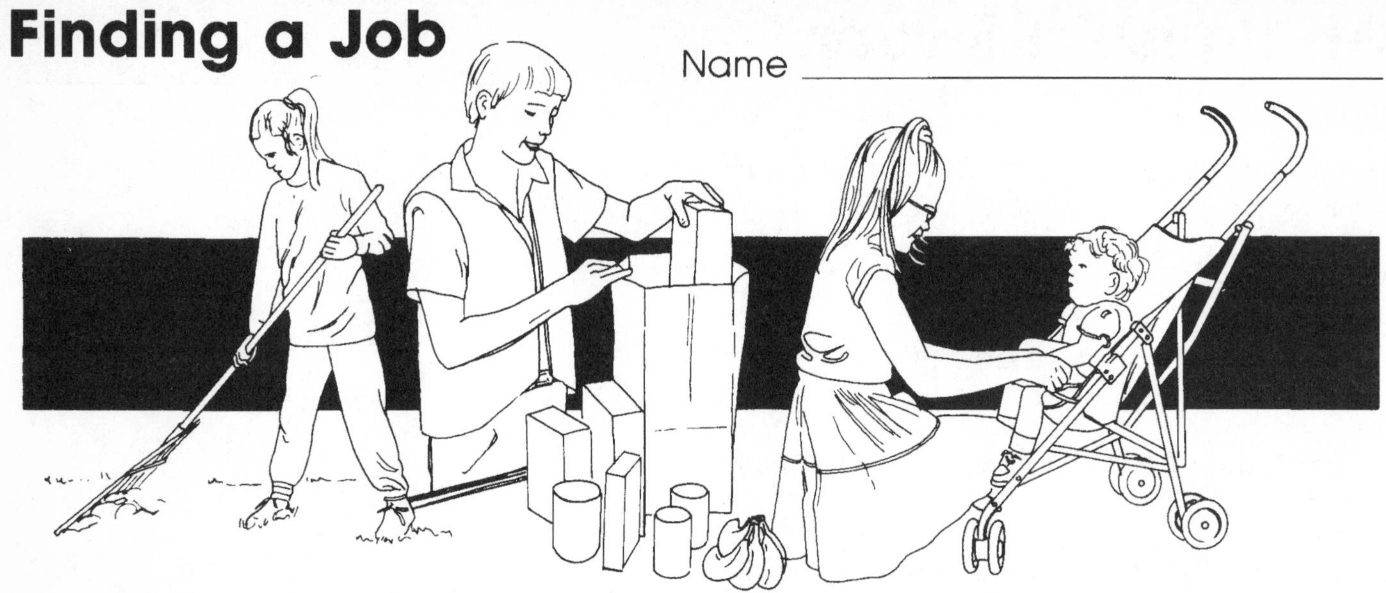

Read through all the statements. Number the instructions in the correct order for finding a job. Cross out the instructions that do not pertain to finding a job.

____ Before you fill out the application, write the information on a piece of scrap paper.

____ Earn some money doing odd jobs around the house and neighborhood.

____ If a prospective employer wants to know more about you than what you put on the application, he or she may call for an interview.

____ Obtain a social security number before you apply for a job.

____ Read want ads and bulletin boards and ask around about available jobs.

____ Look your best when you go for an interview.

____ Put aside a certain amount of money so you will be able to buy the bike you want by the time school begins.

____ Fill out the application legibly in ink.

____ Answer ads with a letter or apply in person.

____ Mail or hand in your application.

____ Figure out what times you are available for work and what sort of work interests you before you begin looking for a job.

____ Earn some money to pay your parents back.

____ Enclose a photocopy of your social security number, a work permit — if required and a picture.

____ Read over your scrap paper and make corrections if necessary.

• Circle the correct word to make the statement true.

The equator is the (longest, shortest) imaginary line that travels around the earth.

United States Time Zones

Name ______________________________

The forty-eight continental United States are divided into four time zones: Eastern, Central, Mountain and Pacific. When you move from east to west, you gain one hour each time you cross into a new time zone.

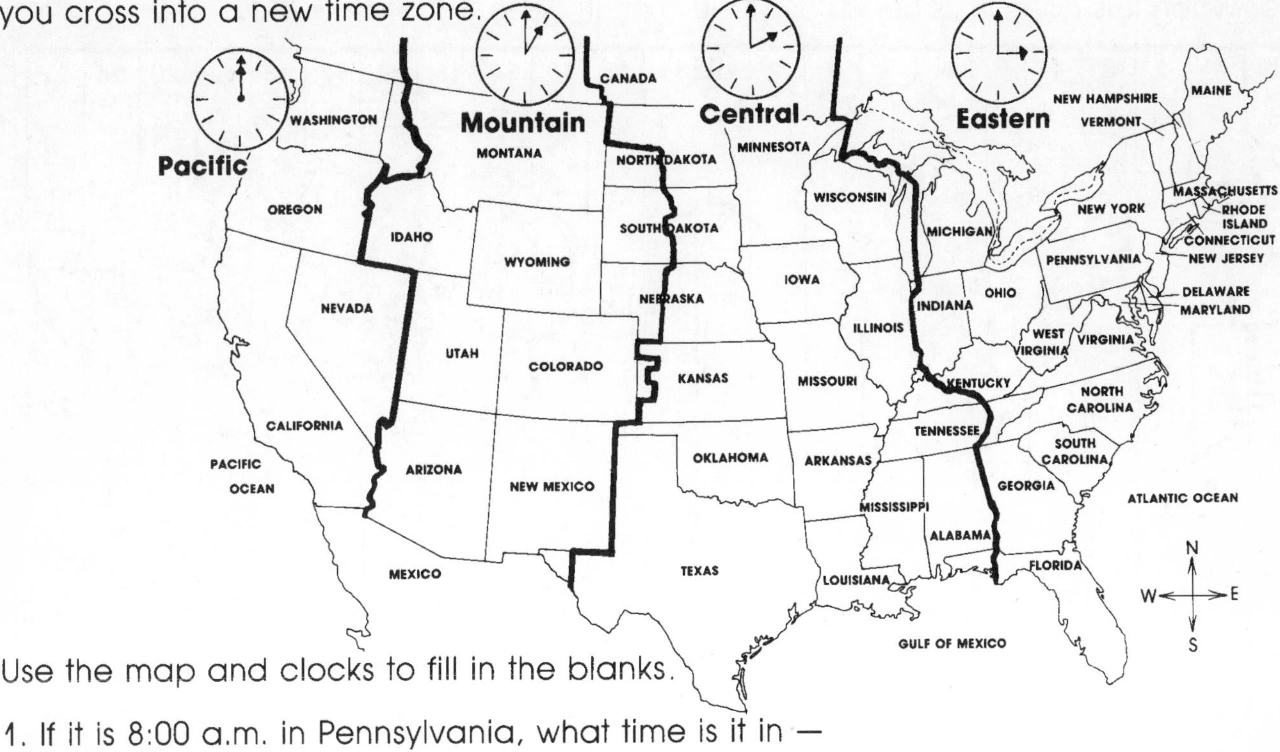

Use the map and clocks to fill in the blanks.

1. If it is 8:00 a.m. in Pennsylvania, what time is it in —
   Mississippi? ________ California? ________ New Mexico? ________ Florida? ________
2. If it is 6:30 p.m. in the state of Washington, what time is it in —
   Washington, D.C.? ________ Wyoming? ________ Nevada? ________ Iowa? ________
3. If it is midnight in Illinois, what time is it in —
   Oregon? ________ Minnesota? ________ most of Montana? ________ Indiana? ________
4. If it is 1:45 a.m. in Arizona, what time is it in —
   Washington? ________ Ohio? ________ Missouri? ________ Utah? ________
5. If you leave North Carolina at 7:00 a.m. and it takes you ten hours to get to Illinois, what time will you arrive in Illinois? ________
6. If you leave Utah at 11:30 a.m. and it takes you one hour to get to Nevada, what time will you arrive in Nevada? ________
7. If you leave Alabama at noon and it takes you two hours to get to South Carolina, what time will you arrive in South Carolina? ________

- Circle the correct word to make the statement true.

President Bush is (older, younger) than President Reagan.

World Time Zones

Name ______________________________

The world is divided into time zones. They are numbered on the map. You will gain one hour each time you cross a time zone going west.

Example: When it is noon in Zone 9, it is 11:00 a.m. in Zone 8 the same day.

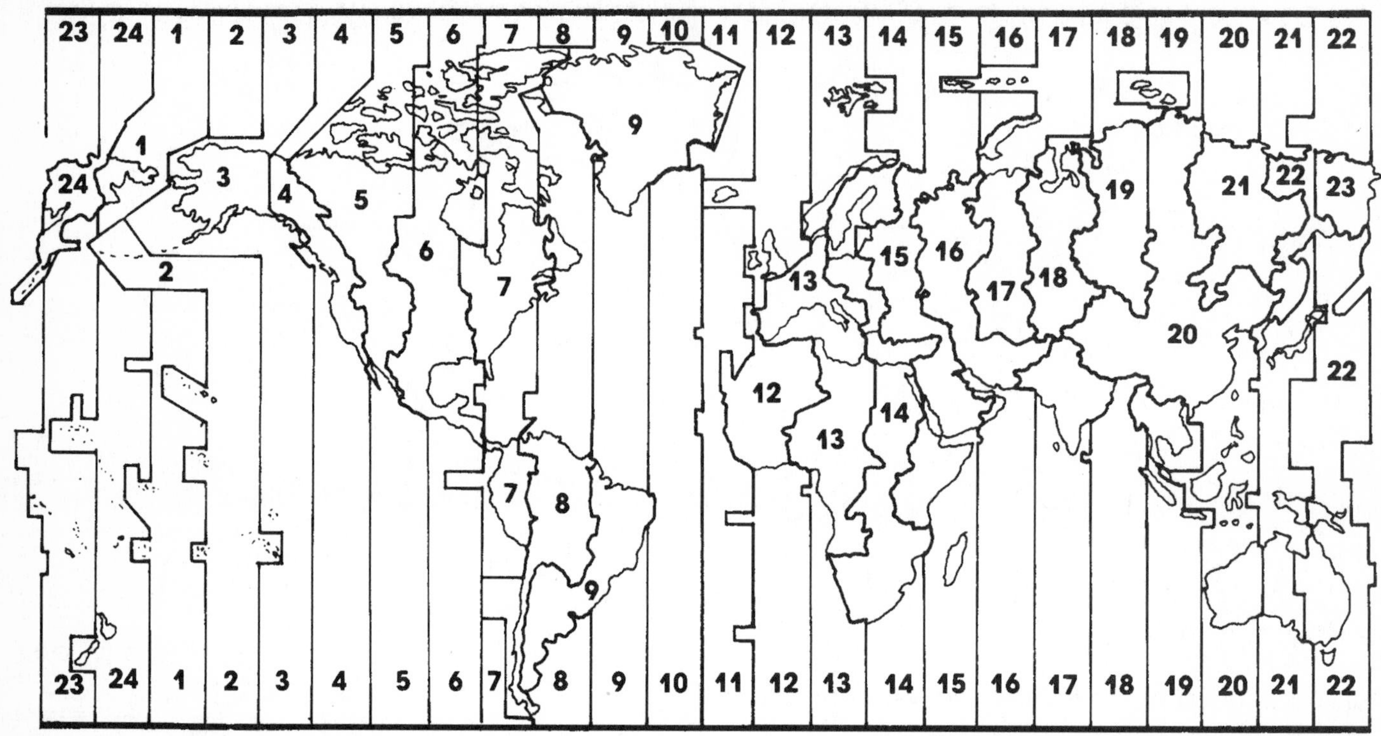

Use the map to fill in the blanks below and circle if it is the day before, the same day, or the day after.

1. If it is 11:00 a.m. in Zone 13, it is ____________________ in Zone 12.
   the day before   the same day   the day after
2. If it is noon in Zone 22, it is ____________________ in Zone 6.
   the day before   the same day   the day after
3. If it is 11:00 p.m. in Zone 7, it is ____________________ in Zone 10.
   the day before   the same day   the day after
4. If it is 1:00 p.m. in Zone 15, it is ____________________ in Zone 24.
   the day before   the same day   the day after
5. If it is 8:00 p.m. in Zone 8, it is ____________________ in Zone 16.
   the day before   the same day   the day after

- Circle the correct word to make the statement true.

  There is a (greater, lesser) distance between Washington D.C. and England than betwee Nome, Alaska and the U.S.S.R.

Time of Action

Name ______________________________

Put an **S** in front of the sentence below if the event happened at the same time. Put an **X** in front if one event happened before the other and draw a line under the event that happened first in each one.

____ The judges for the talent show wrote names on pieces of paper and handed them to the master of ceremonies who announced the winner.

____ Just as I had settled down for the night, there was a knock at the door.

____ All the horses were lined up at the starting gate when the bell rang signaling them to go.

____ When the waitress took our order, we asked her to bring our pop ahead of the meal.

____ The climbers were weary, hungry and cold after they had spent the night on the mountain without any supplies.

____ Mom and Dad fixed up the guest room in a hurry after learning their guests were arriving early.

____ Sparks from the fireplace shot onto the carpet and started a fire.

____ My brother cut the grass and trimmed the hedges while my dad painted the shutters on our house.

____ As the crowd gathered to hear the President, a man's voice announced his arrival.

____ When I suddenly awakened, I discovered my alarm had failed to go off.

____ The stores in the mall open at 10:00 a.m., but the mall opens for walkers at 6:00 a.m.

____ I turned in my report ahead of time because I was going to be absent on its due date.

____ Our house was being painted as we moved in.

____ We are having a family reunion after we come back from our trip.

____ Since it was announced that the baby chimp would be on display from 2:00 - 4:00 daily, throngs of people have come to see him.

- Circle the correct word to make the statement true.

Fifty-nine minutes before three is (earlier, later) than ten minutes after two.

Time Is

Name ____________________

Put an S in front of the sentences below if the events happened at the same time. Put an X in front if one happened before the other and draw a line under the event that happened second.

____ The flute player put his mouth on the instrument and waited for the orchestra conductor to direct him to play.

____ Mother left the iron plugged in and caused the iron to burn out.

____ The jury returned a guilty verdict after they weighed all the evidence.

____ As water vapor rises it cools, and then it condenses.

____ The roadblock aided the police in the capture of the escaped prisoners.

____ After World War I ended, the boundaries of several countries changed.

____ The water ran off the land and carried sediment with it.

____ My sister was born the day the President was inaugurated.

____ Some slaves did not want to live as they were, so they escaped to the North before the end of the Civil War.

____ America boycotted the Olympics because they disapproved of Russia's invasion of Afghanistan.

____ The arson squad investigated the cause of the fire that destroyed an apartment house and took three lives.

____ We celebrated my birthday before my dad had to go on a business trip.

____ Mother wrote a note excusing my tardiness because I had to go to the dentist.

____ The noon whistle blew just as the clock in the church struck 12.

____ A battery will produce electricity when its electrodes produce the right chemical reaction.

____ When the river overflowed its banks, the state militia was called to build a wall of sandbags.

____ It is winter in Australia when it is summer in the United States.

____ Logs were loaded onto a truck for transport to a mill where they would be cut into lumber.

____ The ranger talked to the class about the treatment of the park's wildlife before he took them around the park.

- Circle the correct word to make the statement true.

  An octogenarian is (older, younger) than a centenarian.

When Events Happen

Name ____________________________

Put an S in front of the sentences below if the events happened at the same time. Put an X in front if one event happened before the other and draw a line under the event that happened first in each one.

____ The storm that hit during the night knocked out the electricity in the entire community.

____ As Sheila turned the corner, a fire engine raced by with its lights flashing and sirens blaring.

____ After the final curtain came down, the theater was deserted except for the stage crew taking down the set.

____ As the pitcher threw the ball toward home plate, the base runner stole second.

____ After the construction workers cleared a space for the lumber, they unloaded it quickly.

____ Mother prepared the meal before she got dressed for the guests.

____ The man paid for the car with a personal check, but the bank sent it back because of insufficient funds.

____ When the referee blew his whistle, the centers jumped for the ball.

____ My muscles ached after I took a 40-minute aerobic class.

____ We plan to leave in March for Spain, so I am taking Spanish lessons.

____ I had to go to the doctor for a physical exam before I was allowed to try out for the football team.

____ When the dismissal bell rang, there was a rush for the door.

____ Since I saw you last, I cut my hair.

____ The plumber had to go to his truck for a tool when he saw what the problem was.

____ Although the parade didn't start until noon, the crowd began to form at 10:00 A.M.

____ I caught my finger in the latch when I was closing the door.

____ The library closed before I got there.

____ The cowboy won $100 in the rodeo, but he had to use it to have his broken arm set.

• Circle the correct word to make the statement true.

The Bill of Rights is at the (beginning, end) of the Constitution.

Breeds of Dogs

Name ______________________________

Find the support sentences at the bottom of the page for each topic sentence. Write them in order under the correct topic sentence.

Scottish terriers were originally raised in the Scottish highlands in the 1800's. ______________________________

____

____

____

The dachshund is known for its long body and short legs. ______________________________

____

____

____

The golden retriever is a medium-sized hunting dog. ______________________________

____

____

____

____

Support Sentences

1. The "Scottie" however is the only one with the official name of Scottish terrier.
2. Its body shape helped it carry out the purpose for which it was bred.
3. Because of the dog's easygoing personality, it also makes a good pet in spite of its size.
4. There are other terriers native to Scotland such as the Skye, cairn and West Highland.
5. It is intelligent and easily trained for field work.
6. Its name is German for badger hound.
7. It was originally bred in Germany to hunt badgers.
8. Not only does this dog work well in the field, but it also performs well as a guide for the blind.
9. It is more commonly called, "Scottie."

- Circle the correct word to make the statement true.

  The two sides carried on a (prologue, epilogue, dialogue) into the night to try to settle the labor dispute.

Stonehenge

Name ______________________________

The story is missing some of its sentences. Find them in the box below and write them in the story where they belong.

Few ancient remains that were buried in northern Europe are there today. ____________

____

____

Therefore, less is known about the people of Europe than of inhabitants of other ancient lands. No books have been found, so archeologists do not know if early Europeans could read or write.

____

These monuments show that the Europeans were skilled craftsmen. One of the most impressive of the ancient stone monuments is Stonehenge in southern England. ________

____

____

It is believed that work began on Stonehenge around 2750 B.C. and that it took about 1,000 men to move one vertical stone at a time. They had to be moved from the quarry to their place on the site — a distance of 32 kilometers. ____________________

____

Horizontal stones, or lintels, were then placed all around on top of the vertical ones. It was probably completed around 1500 B.C.

1. It may have been a temple, but most people who have studied it think it might also have been used as a calendar.
2. However, stone monuments were built which did survive.
3. The vertical stones were arranged in a circle.
4. Because the climate is so damp, many things decayed and left little for today's scientists to work with.

- Circle the correct word to make the statement true.

  Brunch is usually served in the (a.m., p.m.)

Forms of Mountain Climbing

Name ______________________

The story is missing some of its sentences. Find them in the box below and write them in the story where they belong.

Mountain climbing is a sport that involves climbing mountains or just hiking in mountain country. ____

Rock climbing involves climbing up rocky slopes. It is popular with beginning climbers because they can practice on cliffs that are not too difficult to climb.

____ Two such pieces are a piton and a snap link. A piton is an iron spike. It is hammered into rock cracks and has a ring at one end from which a rope can be secured. A snap link is a steel clip which attaches a rope to a climber or a piton.

Snow and ice climbers venture out in winter and summer, wherever there are mountains covered with snow and ice. ____

These climbers must also learn to handle ice axes, ice hammers, and ice screws and understand how snow and ice may change under different conditions.

Mixed climbing combines rock climbing with snow and ice climbing. ____ All climbers should be trained and not attempt anything beyond their skill.

1. Rock climbers have special equipment which they must learn to use.
2. Therefore, climbers who participate in mixed climbing must be the very best.
3. There are three basic forms of mountain climbing: rock climbing, snow and ice climbing, and mixed climbing.
4. Snow and ice climbers must learn to use crampons, which are metal spikes attached to boots to grip ice or hard snow.

- Circle the time zone that is two hours behind Eastern Standard Time.

Pacific Standard Time   Mountain Standard Time   Central Standard Time

The Aztecs

Name ______________________________

The story is missing some of its sentences. Find them in the box below and write them in the story where they belong.

The Aztecs were Indians who migrated from the north to Mexico in the twelfth century.

____

____

Much of their civiliation was based on the cultures of tribes in the region ahead of them. ____

____

____

____

Despite their achievements they relied on human beings to do heavy labor as they did not have machinery.

Their capital was built on a huge lake.____

____

They built aqueducts from the mountains to carry clean water to the capital. The wealthier people had homes built of stone and mud bricks. Most farmers lived in huts.

When the Spanish explorers arrived in the early 1500's, they had little trouble overthrowing the Aztecs. ____

____

They aided the Spanish in removing the Aztecs from power. The Aztec civilization disappeared. ____

______________________________________ Some Indians who lived in the area of Mexico City today are descendants of the Aztecs.

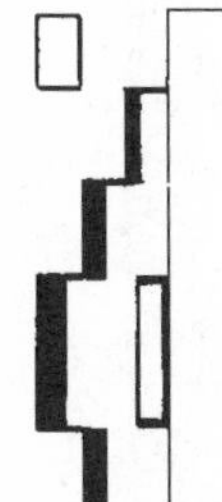

1. They did, however, develop some things of their own such as a stone wheel calendar, a method for weaving cotton, jewelry using semiprecious stones and metalwork.
2. Its capital was leveled and Mexico City was founded on its site.
3. They constructed islands in the middle of the lake on which they built palaces and temples.
4. They were nomadic until they established their own capital, Tenochtitlan.
5. Many of the tribes the Aztecs had conquered resented paying them taxes.

- Circle the correct word to make the statement true.

An appendix is found at the (beginning, middle, end) of a book.

Skill: Ordering a Story

Forensic Medicine

Name ______________________________

The story is missing some of its sentences. Find them in the box below and write them in the story where they belong.

When a dead body is found and the circumstances under which the person died are unknown, the police bring in a medical examiner, a forensic doctor or a scientist. The first thing that must be done is to make an identification of the victim. ______________________

____

______________. There are three basic patterns of fingerprints: a whorl, arch and a loop.

____

____

Fingerprints have always been thought to be the most unique way to identify a person, but a person's teeth are just as distinctive. ______________________________

____

____

Most people have 32 teeth. Each one has several sides from which an identification can be made. ____

____

____

1. By dusting with powder or making a print from an inky pad, fingerprints are made.
2. If a victim is badly burned and fingerprints cannot be taken, identification can be made from his or her teeth.
3. If no papers are on the body, the examiner usually looks for fingerprints.
4. There are also other features such as missing teeth, crooked teeth or false teeth that may help to make an identification.

____

• Circle the correct word to make the statement true.

The Declaration of Independence was written (before, after) the Constitution.

The Sun Dance

Name ______________________________

The story is missing some of its sentences. Find them in the box below and write them in the story where they belong.

The Sun Dance was an important ceremony of the Sioux Indians. The bravest hunters and warriors were offered to the Great Spirit, Wakan'tanka, during the dance. ______

____

The Sun Dance always took place in midsummer when the trees were leaved and the moon was full. ______________________________

____

____

They prayed for good weather. When it was time for the Sun Dance, Indians from far away came to the place of the dance and pitched their tents.

____

First a buffalo skull was placed in the center of the circle facing west. Then one chief stood near the skull and said a prayer to Wakan'tanka. ______________

____

____

When the prayer was over 20 men were chosen to place four sacred 25 foot poles in the center of the circle. As they did, the medicine men led the rest in singing and wishing for a good harvest. ______________________________

____

____

1. The other chiefs sat in a circle around the skull to listen and puff on the peacepipe as it was passed to each one.
2. It was an honor to be chosen for a part in the dance.
3. Finally the dancers, painted blue for sky, red for the sunset, and yellow for lightning, sang and danced for the four sacred poles.
4. Long before the time of the ceremony, medicine men sang, burned sweet grass and offered their pipes to the sky.
5. The Sun Dance began within a great circle of tents.

- Circle the correct word to make the statement true.

The (macroscopic, microscopic) germ was large enough to be seen with the naked eye.

Skill: Ordering a Story

The Pony Express

Name ______________________

Rewrite each paragraph in the correct order.

A rider rode from station to station, approximately 10 to 15 miles apart, where he exchanged his tired horse for a fresh one. The Pony Express was a mail delivery service that operated between St. Joseph, Missouri and Sacramento, California. It consisted of 80 men, 400 horses and 190 stations. A rider's workday usually ended after he had ridden about 75 miles and when he reached a "home" station. From a "home" station another rider relieved him so he could rest.

The Pony Express was the fastest service of its kind at the time. A copy of President Lincoln's first address to Congress was delivered in record time — 7 days and 17 hours. The telegraph could send a message over the wires much faster. It usually carried mail 200 miles a day. The Pony Express only lasted a little over a year because the transcontinental telegraph took its place. Ordinarily it took 10 days or a little less to travel the 1,966-mile route.

• Circle the correct word to make the statement true.

Tom anticipated his punishment (before, after) he lost his homework.

Skill: Ordering a Story

A Submarine Strikes

Name ______________________________

Rewrite each paragraph about a United States Naval battle in a sensible order.

They were the battleships that had fought the United States Navy a few days before. A periscope suddenly popped up through the water in the Pacific Ocean. The captain ordered the crew to be ready for battle. It turned from one side to the other. There were four ships sailing along. It focused on something and stopped.

As the last ship passed, he gave the order to fire. The captain of the U. S. submarine kept an eye on the ships as they passed about ½ mile away. The crew sent four torpedoes toward the enemy ship. No one saw the other torpedoes strike, but they could feel the explosions as they submerged. The captain saw the first torpedo hit. Then the captain shouted, "Dive!" and the sub went under. It hit with such force that the crew on the sub felt the shock.

- Circle the correct word to make the statement true.

  The preface is at the (beginning, middle, end) of a book.

Sea Sagas

Name ______________________

Rewrite each paragraph about a shipwreck in a sensible order.

The ship has been sighted several times drifting without a crew, but it has never been captured. One sea tale tells of a ship trapped by ice off the coast of Alaska during a storm. Could that ghost ship still be sailing in the Arctic seas? When the storm ended the ship was gone. The crew, fearing the ship would be crushed to pieces by the ice, abandoned ship and pitched tents on a nearby beach.

In 1861 the Maritana was wrecked and most of its crew were killed. Some thought that the spirit of a ship lived in its figurehead and would protect the crew from danger. Sailors held several superstitions about the sea. It was the third time a ship bearing that same figurehead sank, but the figurehead remained unharmed. On the other hand, some figureheads were considered unlucky.

• Circle the correct word to make the statement true.

A/An (antecedent, precedent) is set before the fact.

Position and Time

Name ______________________________

Circle the sequence word or words in each sentence. They tell when something happened or position. The first one is done for you.

1. The (ensuing) years were tough on Peter, but his hard work (finally) paid off when he was promoted.
2. The elderly man lived in a remote area, and the welfare people felt he should be moved closer to medical services.
3. When the fledgling completed his first year's training, he became a second-year classman.
4. The inferior paint that was originally used on the shutters chipped off.
5. A primer had to be applied, followed by two new coats of paint.
6. The plumbing in the building was ancient and was replaced with modern copper tubing.
7. My ultimate goal is to graduate at the head of my class.
8. At the outset of the journey the temperature was moderate.
9. The seasoned traveler could not believe it was the ship's maiden voyage.
10. The preliminary results of the test indicated that a slight crack in the car's motor was the cause of the oil leak.
11. When all is said and done, one good friend is better than a lot of acquaintances.
12. Alan did a superior job forecasting the weather.
13. The legislative branch of government is not subordinate to the other two branches of government.
14. The recent news about the dangers of smoking has initiated programs to encourage people to stop smoking.
15. In the long run you are better off working for the camp because you get both free meals and wages.
16. The novice electrician separated the exterior wires from the pole.
17. Seniors sometimes exercise their authority as upperclassmen.
18. There wasn't a single room left in a medium-priced hotel.
19. The train pulled into the terminal 20 minutes behind schedule.
20. The intermediate swimmers were not allowed to swim in the lake until they passed the advanced lifesaving test.
21. It was a trivial matter, but it had to be dealt with immediately.
22. The climax of the play was surprising.
23. The leading lady tripped when she made her entrance.

- Circle the correct word to make the statement true.

  My (ancestors, descendants) are relatives who preceded me.

So What Now?

Name ______________________________

Match the two sentence parts. Write the number of the first part on the line in front of its last part.

1. If you eat food that's good for you
2. If the strange dog bites you
3. If the typewriter breaks down
4. If the fabric begins to fray
5. If the tennis game is canceled
6. If you put the red shirt in with the white sheets
7. If debts are paid promptly
8. If a horse breaks its leg
9. If you brush your teeth after every meal
10. If Mrs. Jones calls for me
11. If there is a storm from the east
12. If there is a heavy snowfall during the winter
13. If the book isn't on the shelf
14. If you have a bug bite
15. If you get the wrong number
16. If there is an electrical storm
17. If there are no objections
18. If there is a fire in a skyscraper
19. If a person is injured
20. If the only lights that go out are in the kitchen
21. If I can't keep the hair out of my eyes
22. If a dollar is worth 100 pennies
23. If you pay in advance for your theater seats

____ sew it around the edge.
____ it should help cut down on your dentistry bills.
____ it's best not to scratch it.
____ check the circuit breakers.
____ you must report it to the rabies control.
____ its runoff may cause rivers to overflow.
____ do not use the elevator.
____ I'm going to tie it back.
____ your bedclothes will turn pink.
____ the rain will seep through our east window.
____ it's best not to talk on the telephone.
____ a person establishes good credit.
____ ask the librarian if it is checked out.
____ tell her I will return soon.
____ dial Information.
____ you will be healthier.
____ it is best not to move him until medical help arrives.
____ there is a fifteen percent reduction.
____ it usually is destroyed.
____ five dollars equal 500 pennies.
____ you will have to write the report by hand.
____ we will continue.
____ I will have to reschedule it.

- Circle the correct word to make the statement true.

  The (primitive, extinct) bird can no longer be found anywhere on Earth.

You Did It

Name ____________________

Write each cause on the line before or after its effect. Each cause will be used only once.

Causes

two of their fellow workers had been fired unnecessarily.
his mother had seen a small creature in her pantry.
they won the state championship.
Since we moved our clocks ahead,
to use to build their winter nests.
there was an unusual amount of rain.
he received the call on his car radio.
to avoid hitting the small boy.
Very little light reached the forest floor through the thick foliage,
After we finished all our work,
the class performed a smelly science experiment.
I go to an aerobic class after work
a fire gutted our home.
they did not like the school's menu.

1. The ball team was given a grand welcome at the airport after ____________________
____
2. The driver swerved his car into a tree ____________________
3. Our flowers blossomed early this year because ____________________
4. The teacher opened all the windows after ____________________
5. The factory workmen were striking because ____________________
____
6. ____________________
____________________ so it was dark and damp.
7. Squirrels ran from tree to tree gathering twigs ____________________
8. ____________________ because it gives me more energy.
9. ____________________ it stays light out later.
10. We bought new furniture after ____________________
11. Most of the class brought their lunch because ____________________
12. The police officer arrived within minutes after ____________________
____
13. Teddy set a trap because ____________________
14. ____________________ father treated us to ice cream.

• Circle the correct word to make the statement true.

A (decathlon, heptathlon) has ten athletic events.

Skill: Predicting Order

Now What?

Name ______________________

Each sentence is either missing a cause or an effect. Find it in the box and add it to the sentence. Next write **C** in front of each sentence to which you added a cause or **E** in front of each one to which an effect was added.

☐ ______________________ a driver should prepare to stop.

☐ The August sun was so blistering hot ______________________

____

☐ When mother cut herself in the kitchen, ______________________

____

☐ ______________________ we went to the movies.

☐ When the bell rang at the end of the first period, ______________________

____

☐ ______________________ my father gets upset.

☐ When juniper is in bloom, ______________________

☐ ______________________ I answered it.

☐ When I opened the door to let the dog in, ______________________

☐ I didn't sleep last night and ______________________

☐ The boy broke his arm when he fell from the tree and ______________________

____

☐ It was so cold out that ______________________

my allergies are very active. the wind blew the lamp over. When the light is yellow, Every time the stock market goes down, The telephone rang and I went to my second-hour class. the doctor put it in a cast. I applied a tourniquet and drove her to the hospital. our pipes froze. I'm tired today. that the grass turned as yellow as straw. There was nothing good on television, so

- Circle the correct word to make the statement true.

  The man had a premonition that something would go wrong (after, before) it happened.

America's First in Space

Name ______________________________

Read the story.

Alan Shepard was born in New Hampshire in 1923. He graduated from the United States Naval Academy in 1944 and served on a destroyer during World War II. After the war he took flight training and became a test pilot. He was an aircraft readiness officer in 1959 at Atlantic Fleet Headquarters when he was chosen to be one of America's original seven astronauts.

He piloted his Mercury space capsule — Freedom 7 — 117 miles into space, landing 302 miles out in the Atlantic Ocean on America's first space flight, May 5, 1961. He received the Distinguished Flying Cross and the Distinguished Service Medal of the National Aeronautics and Space Administration (NASA) for his first space flight.

He was grounded in 1963 because of an inner-ear problem, but when surgery corrected the problem in 1969, he was again allowed to fly. In 1971 he commanded Apollo 14, the third landing on the moon. He was the fifth astronaut on the moon. After that flight he served as chief of the astronaut office at the Johnson Space Center until his retirement. He resigned from the astronaut program and the Navy in 1974 with the rank of rear admiral.

Fill in the time line with the events that occurred during the years given.

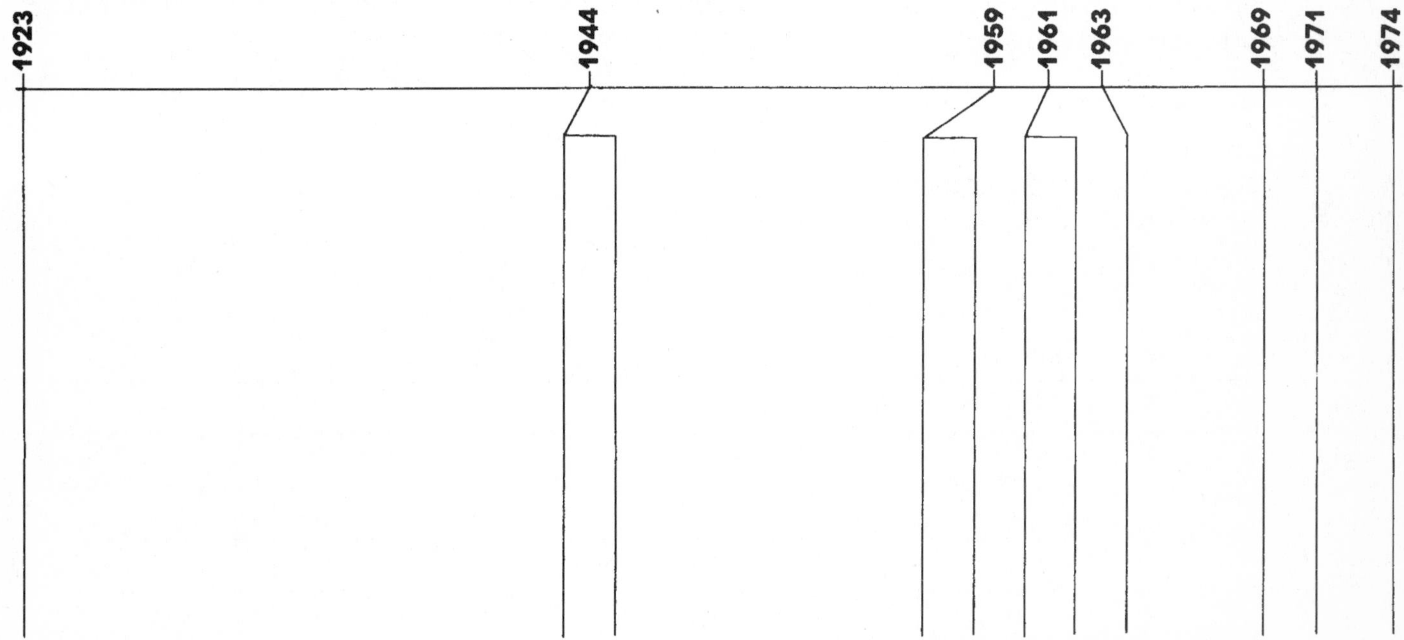

• Circle the amount that is the smallest.

least little less smaller

Horse Racing

Name ______________________________

Make an outline of each paragraph using the statements below each one.

The Kentucky Derby is the most famous horse race in America. It is held every year on the first Saturday in May at Churchill Downs racetrack in Louisville, Kentucky. Only three-year-old horses are eligible to run in the 1¼-mile race. All the male horses running in the Derby carry 126 pounds and the female horses carry 121 pounds.

1¼-mile race
Three-year-old horses
Kentucky Derby
First Saturday of May
Most famous American horse race
Churchill Downs in Louisville

I. ______________________________
   A. ______________________________
   B. ______________________________
   C. ______________________________
   D. ______________________________
   E. ______________________________

The Grand National is the world's most famous steeplechase horse race. It takes place near Liverpool, England every year. The horses must be six years old to enter this difficult 4-mile race. The course is so difficult that often many entries do not finish.

Grand National
Difficult course
World's most famous steeplechase
Six-year-old horses
England every year
4 miles

II. ______________________________
   A. ______________________________
   B. ______________________________
   C. ______________________________
   D. ______________________________
   E. ______________________________

- Circle the correct word to make the statement true.

  The reproduction was made (first, second).

Spiders

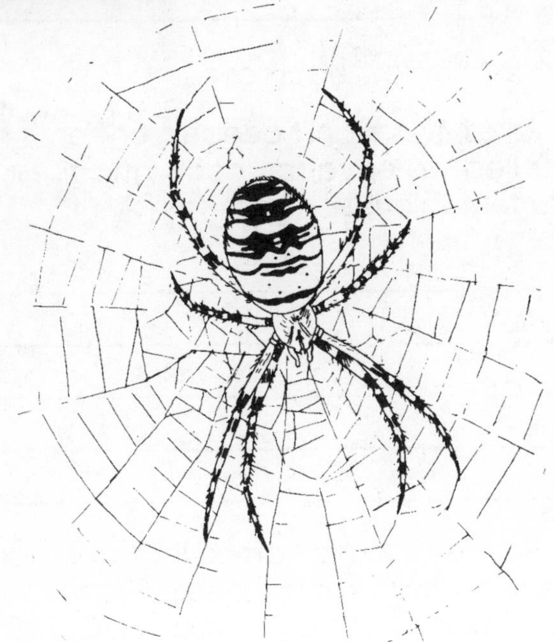

Name ______________________

Make an outline of the article about spiders using the statements below.

Spiders are various sizes, shapes and colors. Some are smaller than a pin's head. Others are the size of a hand. Most spiders are brown, black, or gray, but some are beautifully colored. A spider is not an insect, but rather an arachnid with eight legs.

Spiders live wherever there is food. They may live inside or outside of buildings. They may live below water or in high altitudes.

All spiders spin silk, but not all spiders spin webs. Those that do use them to catch insects for food. A spider's web is very strong and an insect seldom escapes from its sticky threads.

Spiders are more of a friend to man than an enemy. They eat insects that destroy crops and carry diseases that are harmful to humans. Some spiders capture and eat each other, and some also eat larger animals such as mice. There are only six kinds of spiders in North America that are harmful to humans, but their bites seldom cause much distress.

Spiders

Friend to man	I. ______________________
Appearance	A. ______________________
Some spin webs	B. ______________________
Spin	II. ______________________
In water or high altitude	A. ______________________
Eat harmful insects and animals	B. ______________________
Various sizes, shapes, colors	III. ______________________
All spin silk	A. ______________________
Eight legs	B. ______________________
Habitats	IV. ______________________
Most bites not harmful to man	A. ______________________
Inside or outside	B. ______________________

- Circle the correct word to make the statement true.

  A cow's milk comes in (before, after) her calf is born.

Clouds

Name ____________________

Make an outline of each paragraph using the statements below each one.

Clouds form from water that has evaporated from lakes, rivers and oceans, or from plants and moist soil. When the evaporated water, called water vapor, cools and rises, it condenses into water droplets and ice crystals. These form clouds.

Forms water droplets	I. ____________________
Forms ice crystals	A. ____________________
How clouds form	B. ____________________
Water vapor cools, rises and condenses	1. ____________________
Water evaporates on earth	2. ____________________

Clouds come in all shapes and sizes. Scientists have given clouds names that describe their appearance. Clouds that seem to be in layers are called stratus clouds. Clouds that pile on top of one another are cumulus clouds. Cirrus clouds are high and curly. Clouds continually change their shapes as they come in contact with the air and action of the wind.

Cirrus	II. ____________________
Appearance of clouds	A. ____________________
Continually change shape	1. ____________________
Stratus	2. ____________________
Names	3. ____________________
Cumulus	B. ____________________

Clouds bring different kinds of weather to earth. The rain and snow that drops from them is necessary to all living things. Sometimes, however, clouds bring weather that is not very helpful. Tornadoes and hail can both cause a lot of damage.

Hail	III. ____________________
Necessary	A. ____________________
Tornadoes	1. ____________________
Snow	2. ____________________
Clouds bring different weather	B. ____________________
Rain	1. ____________________
Destructive	2. ____________________

- Circle the correct word to make the statement true.

  Third is a/an (ordinal, cardinal) number.

What a Day!

Name ______________________________

Write a story following the order of the outline.

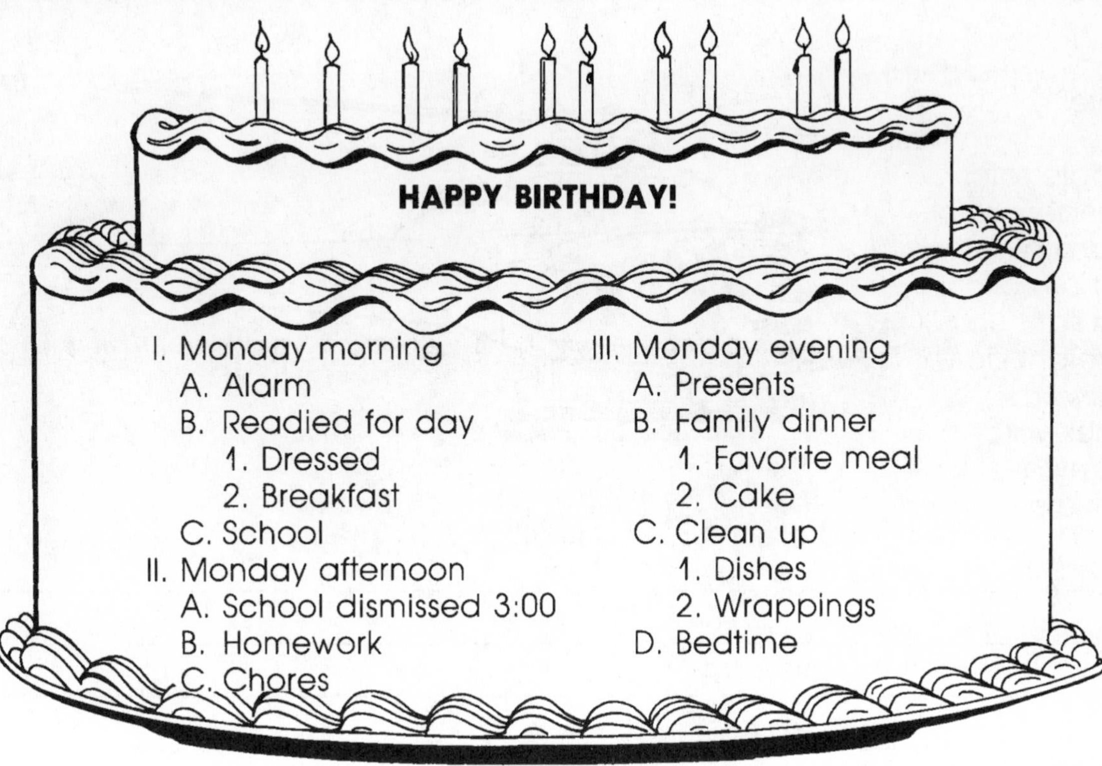

____

____

____

____

____

____

____

____

____

____

____

____

____

- Circle the correct word to make the statement true.

  The baby robins (expired, hatched) from their eggs three weeks after the first one was laid.

Scientific Tidbits

Name ______________________________

Write a short paragraph for each outline. Make sure each one follows the order of the outline.

I. Helicopter
   A. Types
      1. Single rotor
      2. Tandem rotor
      3. Coaxial rotor
   B. Flight directions
      1. Straight up
      2. Straight down
      3. Forward
      4. Backward
      5. Sideways
      6. Hovers

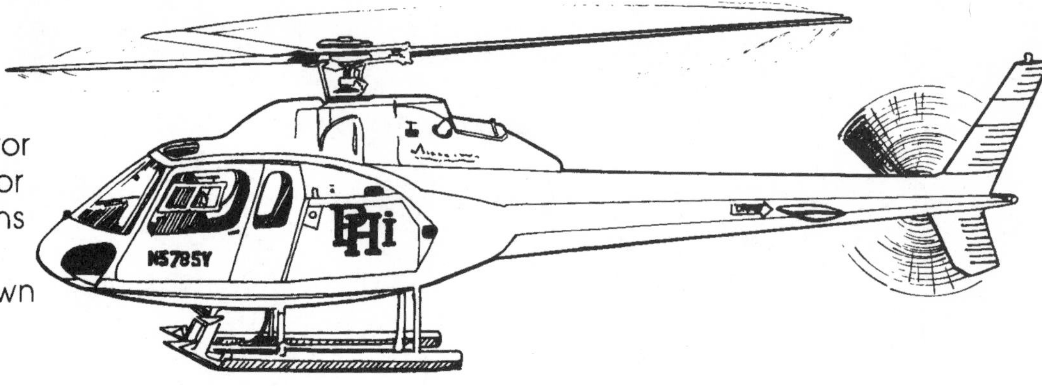

____

____

____

____

____

____

I. Lava
   A. Inside earth
      1. Molten rock
      2. Travels along cracks in earth
   B. On earth's surface
      1. Very hot at first
      2. Cools quickly

____

____

____

____

____

____

- Circle the correct word to make the statement true.

  9 ones and 8 tens are (greater, less) than 9 tens and 8 ones.

Mound Builders

Name ________________________________

The story below contains four sets of parentheses to show where sentences are missing. Find the missing sentences at the end of the story. Write the number of each missing sentence in the parentheses where it belongs.

Mound Builders were various groups of prehistoric American Indians. Some built mounds of earth to be used as burial places, and others used them as platforms to hold temples and lodges. The earthen mounds were mostly built between 600 B.C. and A.D. 1500 ( ) There were no animals or machinery to do the work for them.

There were two cultures that used mounds for burial places. The Adena lived in the Ohio River Valley. They piled dirt over their dead. As more bodies were buried, the size of the mound increased. ( ) It is about seventy feet high. The Adena also built some mounds shaped like animals. The Great Serpent Mound near Hillsboro, Ohio looks like a huge snake from the air. It is about ¼ of a mile from its head to its tail.

The other culture to use mounds for burial were the Hopewell. They were located in what is now Ohio, Indiana, Illinois, Michigan, Wisconsin, Iowa and Missouri. They built many more burial mounds than the Adena. The largest Hopewell site is called Newark Earthworks. It is in Newark, Ohio. ( )

The Mississippian Culture lasted from about A.D. 700 until the 1700's. These Indians built mounds used as bases for temples. They lived in the Mississippi Valley area and along its branches. ( ) Around 40,000 people lived there. Its largest mound, Monk's Mound, had a base larger than the Great Pyramid of Egypt.

1. Cahokia in present-day Illinois was its largest city.
2. The mounds were built by workers who carried loads of dirt on their backs.
3. One of the Adena's largest burial mounds is in Moundsville, West Virginia.
4. It has several large earthen structures surrounded by a ridge.

- Circle the word that means the finest.

better   good   best

Underwater

Name ______________________________

The story below contains five sets of parentheses to show where sentences are missing. Find the missing sentences at the end of the story. Write the number of each sentence in the parentheses where it belongs.

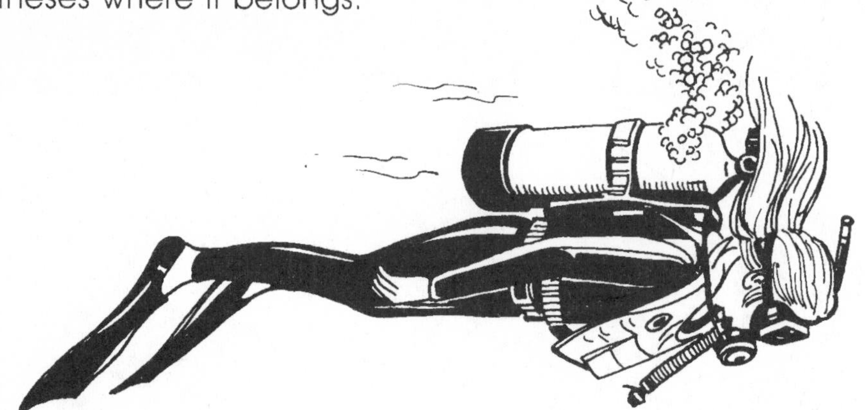

Eugenie Clark was born in New York in 1922. (   ) She spent every Saturday of her childhood at the aquarium watching the fish.

She furthered her interest in water creatures at home. She had a 15-gallon aquarium in her room. (   ) She grew up to be an ichthyologist, a fish scientist.

She earned a bachelor degree in zoology and went on to get a doctorate. Much of her learning took place in the sea, rather than in the classroom. (   ) When she studied blowfish in the South Seas, she practiced free diving. That is, she used only a mask, fins and a snorkel. She studied poisonous fish in the Red Sea and the gulf waters, and other marine life off the west coast of Florida.

Sharks became Eugenie's main interest when she was in Florida. (   ) She taught the sharks to push a target and ring a bell in order to get food as a reward. She trained them to choose between targets of different designs and colors. She observed shark behavior and concluded that they seemed more likely to attack during early morning and late afternoon hours. She became an authority on shark behavior. She has written books about her work and has received numerous awards for it.

She is not often recognized for what she did because it really is not in an ichthyologist's field. In 1959 when she was working off Florida's coast, she and her fellow worker found prehistoric Indian bones. (   )

1. From the age of nine, when her mother first dropped her off at the city's aquarium, she was interested in marine life.
2. She reported their discovery of an ancient human skull which contained the oldest preserved brain known to man.
3. She had fish, toads, salamanders and alligators in her collection.
4. She caught and studied over 2,000 of them.
5. She took up hard hat diving when she worked for a well-known ichthyologist and mammalogist who was studying the water off the coast of southern California.

- Circle the correct word to make the statement true.

  Lincoln freed the slaves (before, after) Washington was President.

Tutankhamen

Name ______________________________

The story below contains five sets of parentheses to show where sentences are missing. Find the missing sentences at the end of the story. Write the number of each missing sentence in the parentheses where it belongs.

The Valley of the Kings is located on barren desert land in Egypt, about 350 miles south of Cairo. ( ) Between 1550 and 1100 B.C. many kings were buried in the barren valley. Their treasures were buried with them.

The exact location of each kings' tomb was meant to be a secret. The kings hired guards to watch the tombs, but when the money ran out the tombs were left unguarded. The guards may have even joined tomb robbers in the removal of the king's treasures. ( ) Every tomb that was entered by these travelers was later found emptied of its contents.

One king's tomb was so well hidden that the grave robbers never found it. ( ) Howard Carter and Lord Carnarvon opened the door to find the greatest treasure ever found in a tomb. King Tut's tomb was made up of four rooms. ( ) The mummy of King Tut was found in one room.

( ) He was not one of Egypt's great rulers. His fame has come from the treasures he left behind. The kings who ruled with power and for greater periods of time probably had many more treasures buried with them. But their tombs were robbed, and so were we — from knowing what they had. However, King Tut's splendid treasures may be viewed in the Cairo Museum to give us an idea of life during Egypt's Middle Kingdom.

1. Jewelry, clothing and furniture were in each room.
2. Thousands of years passed before the tombs were discovered by foreign travelers.
3. Study of the mummy suggests the king was perhaps 19 years old when he died.
4. It was used as a cemetery by the Pharaohs.
5. Not until 1922, when two Englishmen found a hidden staircase covered by debris, was King Tut, or Tutankhamen's tomb found.

- Circle the correct word to make the statement true.

An average is the (top, middle, bottom) figure.

Answer Key

Sequencing

Grade 6

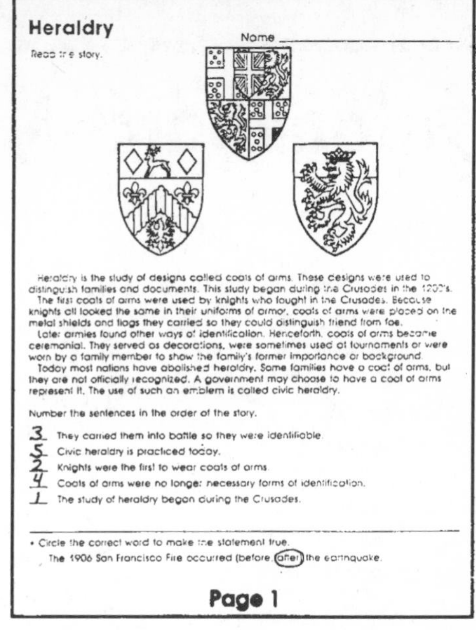

Heraldry Name ____________

Read the story.

Heraldry is the study of designs called coats of arms. These designs were used to distinguish families and documents. This study began during the Crusades in the 1200's.
The first coats of arms were used by knights who fought in the Crusades. Because knights all looked the same in their uniforms of armor, coats of arms were placed on the metal shields and flags they carried so they could distinguish friend from foe.
Later armies found other ways of identification. Henceforth, coats of arms became ceremonial. They served as decorations, were sometimes used at tournaments or were worn by a family member to show the family's former importance or background.
Today most nations have abolished heraldry. Some families have a coat of arms, but they are not officially recognized. A government may choose to have a coat of arms represent it. The use of such an emblem is called civic heraldry.

Number the sentences in the order of the story.

3 They carried them into battle so they were identifiable.
5 Civic heraldry is practiced today.
2 Knights were the first to wear coats of arms.
4 Coats of arms were no longer necessary forms of identification.
1 The study of heraldry began during the Crusades.

• Circle the correct word to make the statement true.
The 1906 San Francisco Fire occurred (before, **after**) the earthquake.

Page 1

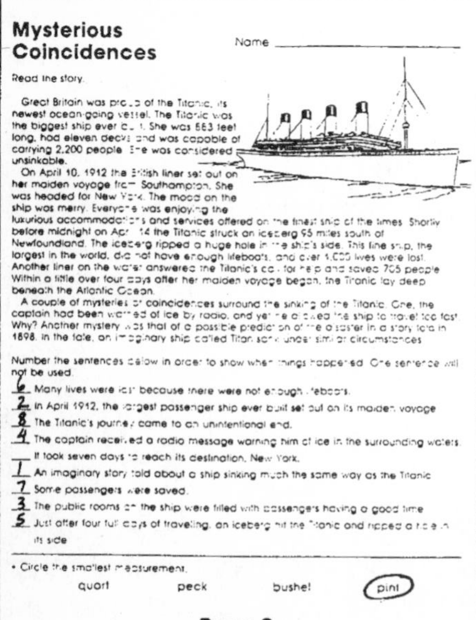

Mysterious Coincidences Name ____________

Read the story.

Great Britain was proud of the Titanic, its newest ocean-going vessel. The Titanic was the biggest ship ever built. She was 883 feet long, had eleven decks and was capable of carrying 2,200 people. She was considered unsinkable.
On April 10, 1912 the British liner set out on her maiden voyage from Southampton. She was headed for New York. The mood on the ship was merry. Everyone was enjoying the luxurious accommodations and services offered on the finest ship of the times. Shortly before midnight on April 14 the Titanic struck an iceberg 95 miles south of Newfoundland. The iceberg ripped a huge hole in the ship's side. This fine ship, the largest in the world, did not have enough lifeboats, and over 1,500 lives were lost. Another liner on the water answered the Titanic's call for help and saved 705 people. Within a little over four days after her maiden voyage began, the Titanic lay deep beneath the Atlantic Ocean.
A couple of mysteries or coincidences surround the sinking of the Titanic. One, the captain had been warned of ice by radio, and yet he allowed the ship to travel too fast. Why? Another mystery was that of a possible prediction of the disaster in a story told in 1898. In the tale, an imaginary ship called Titan sank under similar circumstances.

Number the sentences below in order to show when things happened. One sentence will not be used.

6 Many lives were lost because there were not enough lifeboats.
2 In April 1912, the largest passenger ship ever built set out on its maiden voyage.
8 The Titanic's journey came to an unintentional end.
4 The captain received a radio message warning him of ice in the surrounding waters.
__ It took seven days to reach its destination, New York.
1 An imaginary story told about a ship sinking much the same way as the Titanic.
7 Some passengers were saved.
3 The public rooms on the ship were filled with passengers having a good time.
5 Just after four full days of traveling, an iceberg hit the Titanic and ripped a hole in its side.

• Circle the smallest measurement.
quart peck bushel **pint**

Page 2

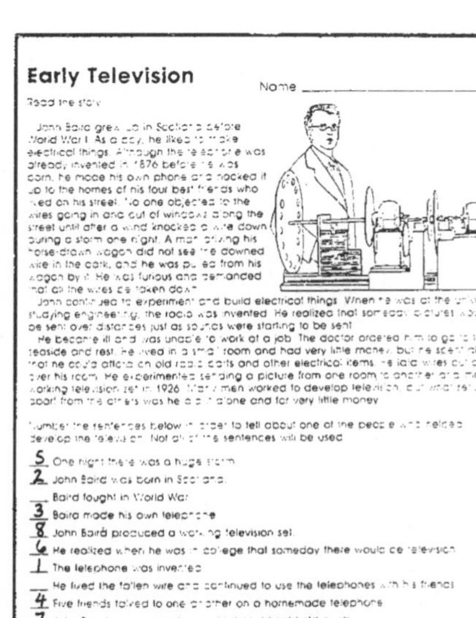

Early Television Name ____________

Read the story.

John Baird grew up in Scotland before World War I. As a boy, he liked to make electrical things. Although the telephone was already invented in 1876 before he was born, he made his own phone and hooked it up to the homes of his four best friends who lived on his street. No one objected to the wires going in and out of windows along the street until after a wind knocked a wire down during a storm one night. A man driving his horse-drawn wagon did not see the downed wire in the dark, and he was pulled from his wagon by it. He was furious and demanded that all the wires be taken down.
John continued to experiment and build electrical things. When he was at the university studying engineering, the radio was invented. He realized that someday pictures would be sent over distances just as sounds were starting to be sent.
He became ill and was unable to work at a job. The doctor ordered him to go to the seaside and rest. He lived in a small room and had very little money, but he scientist that he could afford an old radio, parts and other electrical items. He laid wires out all over his room. He experimented sending a picture from one room to another and made a working television set in 1926. Many men worked to develop television, but what set John apart from the others was he did it alone and for very little money.

Number the sentences below in order to tell about one of the people who helped develop the television. Not all of the sentences will be used.

5 One night there was a huge storm.
2 John Baird was born in Scotland.
__ Baird fought in World War I.
3 Baird made his own telephone.
8 John Baird produced a working television set.
6 He realized when he was in college that someday there would be television.
1 The telephone was invented.
__ He lived the fallen wire and continued to use the telephones with his friends.
4 Five friends talked to one another on a homemade telephone.
7 John Baird was in poor health and could not hold a job.

• Circle the highest temperature.
150°F **100°C** 200°F

Page 3

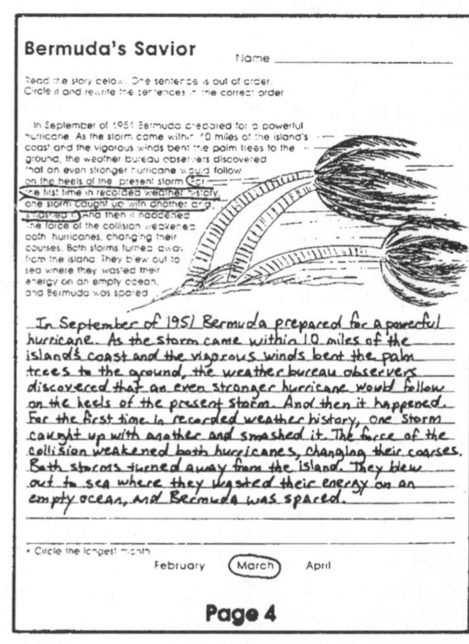

Bermuda's Savior Name ____________

Read the story below. One sentence is out of order. Circle it and rewrite the sentences in the correct order.

In September of 1951 Bermuda prepared for a powerful hurricane. As the storm came within 10 miles of the island's coast and the vigorous winds bent the palm trees to the ground, the weather bureau observers discovered that an even stronger hurricane would follow on the heels of the present storm. For the first time in recorded weather history, one storm caught up with another and smashed it. And then it happened. The force of the collision weakened both hurricanes, changing their courses. Both storms turned away from the island. They blew out to sea where they wasted their energy on an empty ocean, and Bermuda was spared.

In September of 1951 Bermuda prepared for a powerful hurricane. As the storm came within 10 miles of the island's coast and the vigorous winds bent the palm trees to the ground, the weather bureau observers discovered that an even stronger hurricane would follow on the heels of the present storm. And then it happened. For the first time in recorded weather history, one storm caught up with another and smashed it. The force of the collision weakened both hurricanes, changing their courses. Both storms turned away from the island. They blew out to sea where they wasted their energy on an empty ocean, and Bermuda was spared.

• Circle the longest month.
February **March** April

Page 4

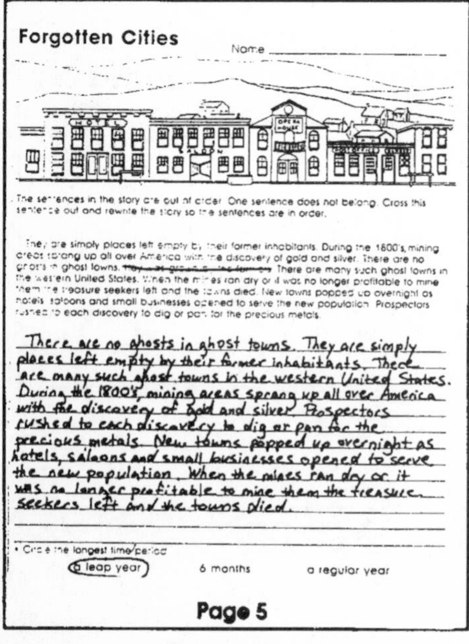

Forgotten Cities Name ____________

The sentences in the story are out of order. One sentence does not belong. Cross this sentence out and rewrite the story so the sentences are in order.

They are simply places left empty by their former inhabitants. During the 1800's mining areas sprang up all over America with the discovery of gold and silver. There are no ghosts in ghost towns. ~~They are great places for fun.~~ There are many such ghost towns in the western United States. When the mines ran dry or it was no longer profitable to mine them the treasure seekers left and the towns died. New towns popped up overnight as hotels, saloons and small businesses opened to serve the new population. Prospectors rushed to each discovery to dig or pan for the precious metals.

There are no ghosts in ghost towns. They are simply places left empty by their former inhabitants. There are many such ghost towns in the western United States. During the 1800's, mining areas sprang up all over America with the discovery of gold and silver. Prospectors rushed to each discovery to dig or pan for the precious metals. New towns popped up overnight as hotels, saloons and small businesses opened to serve the new population. When the mines ran dry or it was no longer profitable to mine them the treasure seekers left and the towns died.

• Circle the longest time period.
a leap year 6 months a regular year

Page 5

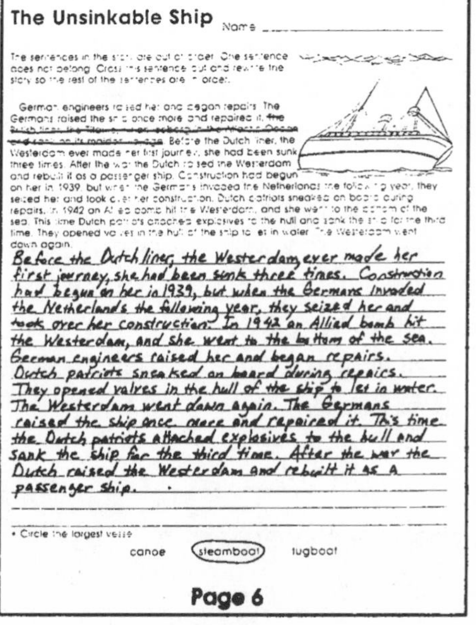

The Unsinkable Ship Name ____________

The sentences in the story are out of order. One sentence does not belong. Cross this sentence out and rewrite the story so the rest of the sentences are in order.

German engineers raised her and began repairs. The Germans raised the ship once more and repaired it. ~~The Dutch liner, the Titanic, hit an iceberg in the Atlantic Ocean on her maiden voyage.~~ Before the Dutch liner, the Westerdam ever made her first journey, she had been sunk three times. After the war the Dutch raised the Westerdam and rebuilt it as a passenger ship. Construction had begun on her in 1939, but when the Germans invaded the Netherlands the following year, they seized her and took over her construction. Dutch patriots sneaked on board during repairs. In 1942 an Allied bomb hit the Westerdam, and she went to the bottom of the sea. This time Dutch patriots attached explosives to the hull and sank the ship for the third time. They opened valves in the hull of the ship to let in water. The Westerdam went down again.

Before the Dutch liner, the Westerdam ever made her first journey, she had been sunk three times. Construction had begun on her in 1939, but when the Germans invaded the Netherlands the following year, they seized her and took over her construction. In 1942 an Allied bomb hit the Westerdam, and she went to the bottom of the sea. German engineers raised her and began repairs. Dutch patriots sneaked on board during repairs. They opened valves in the hull of the ship to let in water. The Westerdam went down again. The Germans raised the ship once more and repaired it. This time the Dutch patriots attached explosives to the hull and sank the ship for the third time. After the war the Dutch raised the Westerdam and rebuilt it as a passenger ship.

• Circle the largest vessel.
canoe **steamboat** tugboat

Page 6

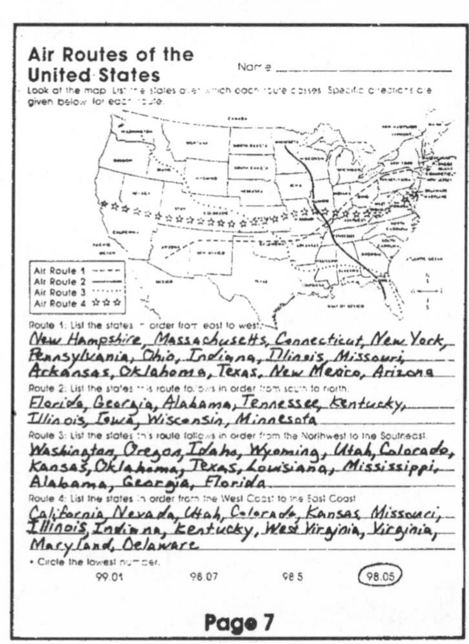

Air Routes of the United States Name ____________

Look at the map. List the states over which each route passes. Specific directions are given below for each route.

Route 1: List the states in order from east to west.
New Hampshire, Massachusetts, Connecticut, New York, Pennsylvania, Ohio, Indiana, Illinois, Missouri, Arkansas, Oklahoma, Texas, New Mexico, Arizona

Route 2: List the states this route follows in order from south to north.
Florida, Georgia, Alabama, Tennessee, Kentucky, Illinois, Iowa, Wisconsin, Minnesota

Route 3: List the states this route follows in order from the Northwest to the Southeast.
Washington, Oregon, Idaho, Wyoming, Utah, Colorado, Kansas, Oklahoma, Texas, Louisiana, Mississippi, Alabama, Georgia, Florida

Route 4: List the states in order from the West Coast to the East Coast.
California, Nevada, Utah, Colorado, Kansas, Missouri, Illinois, Indiana, Kentucky, West Virginia, Virginia, Maryland, Delaware

• Circle the lowest number.
99.01 98.07 98.5 **98.05**

Page 7

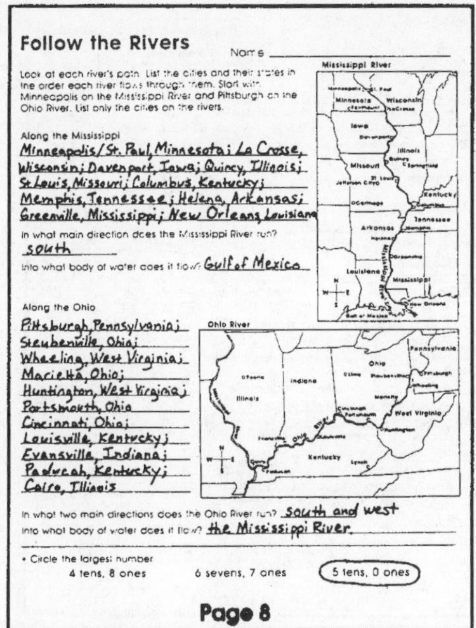

Follow the Rivers

Name

Look at each river's path. List the cities and their states in the order each river flows through them. Start with Minneapolis on the Mississippi River and Pittsburgh on the Ohio River. List only the cities on the rivers.

Along the Mississippi

Minneapolis/St. Paul, Minnesota; La Crosse, Wisconsin; Davenport, Iowa; Quincy, Illinois; St. Louis, Missouri; Columbus, Kentucky; Memphis, Tennessee; Helena, Arkansas; Greenville, Mississippi; New Orleans, Louisiana

In what main direction does the Mississippi River run? south

Into what body of water does it flow? Gulf of Mexico

Along the Ohio

Pittsburgh, Pennsylvania; Steubenville, Ohio; Wheeling, West Virginia; Marietta, Ohio; Huntington, West Virginia; Portsmouth, Ohio; Cincinnati, Ohio; Louisville, Kentucky; Evansville, Indiana; Paducah, Kentucky; Cairo, Illinois

In what two main directions does the Ohio River run? South and west

Into what body of water does it flow? the Mississippi River

• Circle the largest number

4 tens, 8 ones   6 sevens, 7 ones   (5 tens, 0 ones)

Page 8

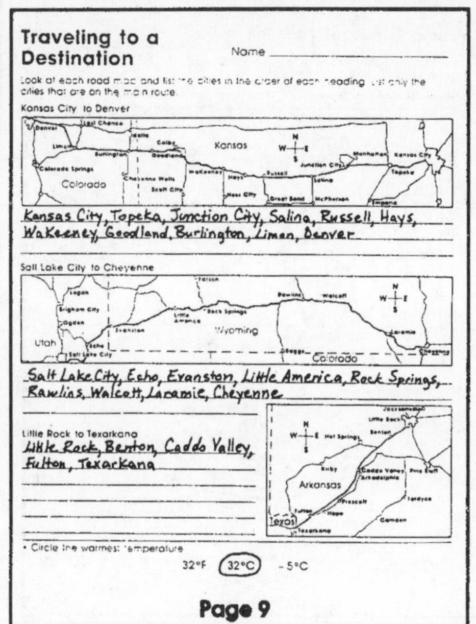

Traveling to a Destination

Name

Look at each road map and list the cities in the order of each heading. List only the cities that are on the main route.

Kansas City to Denver

Kansas City, Topeka, Junction City, Salina, Russell, Hays, WaKeeney, Goodland, Burlington, Limon, Denver

Salt Lake City to Cheyenne

Salt Lake City, Echo, Evanston, Little America, Rock Springs, Rawlins, Walcott, Laramie, Cheyenne

Little Rock to Texarkana

Little Rock, Benton, Caddo Valley, Fulton, Texarkana

• Circle the warmest temperature

32°F   (32°C)   -5°C

Page 9

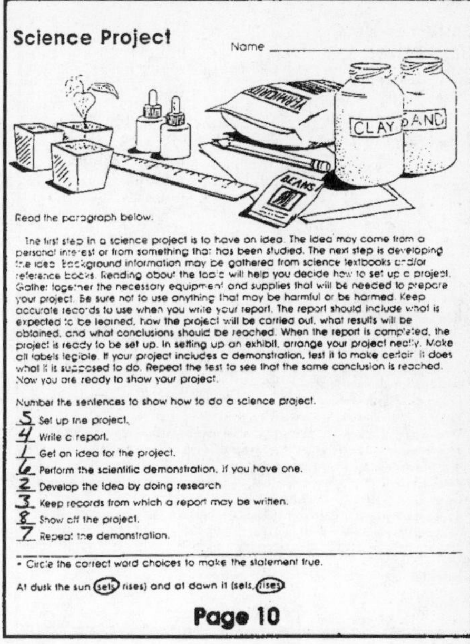

Science Project

Name

Read the paragraph below.

The first step in a science project is to have an idea. The idea may come from a personal interest or from something that has been studied. The next step is developing the idea. Background information may be gathered from science textbooks and/or reference books. Reading about the topic will help you decide how to set up a project. Gather together the necessary equipment and supplies that will be needed to prepare your project. Be sure not to use anything that may be harmful or be harmed. Keep accurate records to use when you write your report. The report should include what is expected to be learned, how the project will be carried out, what results will be obtained, and what conclusions should be reached. When the report is completed, the project is ready to be set up. In setting up an exhibit, arrange your project neatly. Make all labels legible. If your project includes a demonstration, test it to make certain it does what it is supposed to do. Repeat the test to see that the same conclusion is reached. Now you are ready to show your project.

Number the sentences to show how to do a science project.

5 Set up the project.
4 Write a report.
1 Get an idea for the project.
6 Perform the scientific demonstration, if you have one.
2 Develop the idea by doing research.
3 Keep records from which a report may be written.
8 Show off the project.
7 Repeat the demonstration.

• Circle the correct word choices to make the statement true.

At dusk the sun (sets, rises) and at dawn it (sets, rises).

Page 10

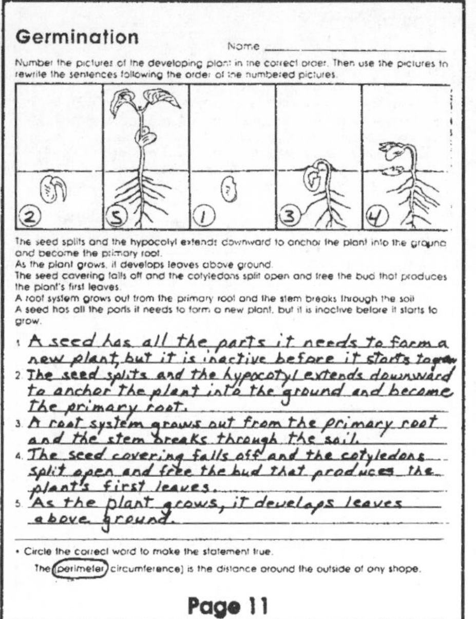

Germination

Name

Number the pictures of the developing plant in the correct order. Then use the pictures to rewrite the sentences following the order of the numbered pictures.

2 5 1 3 4

The seed splits and the hypocotyl extends downward to anchor the plant into the ground and become the primary root.
As the plant grows, it develops leaves above ground.
The seed covering falls off and the cotyledons split open and free the bud that produces the plant's first leaves.
A root system grows out from the primary root and the stem breaks through the soil.
A seed has all the parts it needs to form a new plant, but it is inactive before it starts to grow.

1. A seed has all the parts it needs to form a new plant, but it is inactive before it starts to grow.
2. The seed splits and the hypocotyl extends downward to anchor the plant into the ground and become the primary root.
3. A root system grows out from the primary root and the stem breaks through the soil.
4. The seed covering falls off and the cotyledons split open and free the bud that produces the plant's first leaves.
5. As the plant grows, it develops leaves above ground.

• Circle the correct word to make the statement true.

The (perimeter, circumference) is the distance around the outside of any shape.

Page 11

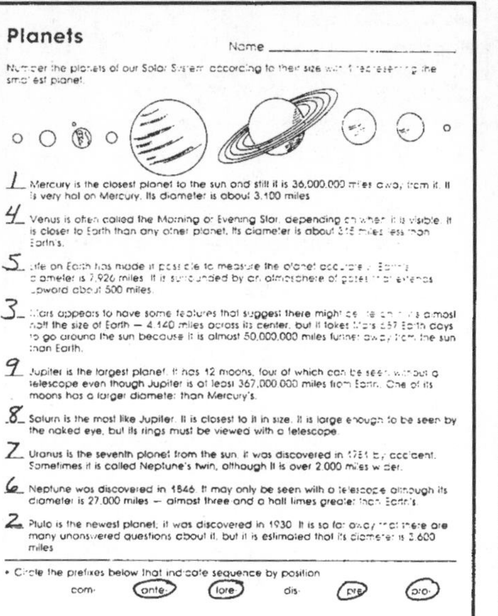

Planets

Name

Number the planets of our Solar System according to their size with 1 representing the smallest planet.

1 Mercury is the closest planet to the sun and still it is 36,000,000 miles away from it. It is very hot on Mercury. Its diameter is about 3,100 miles.

4 Venus is often called the Morning or Evening Star, depending on when it is visible. It is closer to Earth than any other planet. Its diameter is about 315 miles less than Earth's.

5 Life on Earth has made it possible to measure the planet accurately. Earth's diameter is 7,926 miles. It is surrounded by an atmosphere of gases that extends upward about 500 miles.

3 Mars appears to have some features that suggest there might be life on it. It is almost half the size of Earth — 4,140 miles across its center, but it takes Mars 687 Earth days to go around the sun because it is almost 50,000,000 miles further away from the sun than Earth.

9 Jupiter is the largest planet. It has 12 moons, four of which can be seen without a telescope even though Jupiter is at least 367,000,000 miles from Earth. One of its moons has a larger diameter than Mercury's.

8 Saturn is the most like Jupiter. It is closest to it in size. It is large enough to be seen by the naked eye, but its rings must be viewed with a telescope.

7 Uranus is the seventh planet from the sun. It was discovered in 1781 by accident. Sometimes it is called Neptune's twin, although it is over 2,000 miles wider.

6 Neptune was discovered in 1846. It may only be seen with a telescope although its diameter is 27,000 miles — almost three and a half times greater than Earth's.

2 Pluto is the newest planet; it was discovered in 1930. It is so far away that there are many unanswered questions about it, but it is estimated that its diameter is 3,600 miles.

• Circle the prefixes below that indicate sequence by position

com-   (ante-)   (fore-)   dis-   (pre-)   (pro-)

Page 12

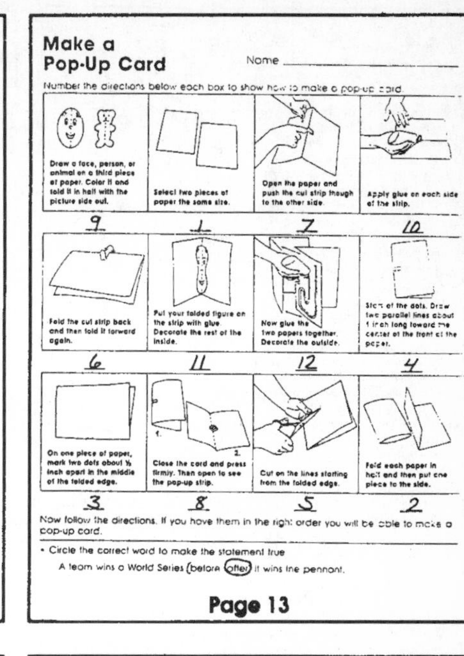

Make a Pop-Up Card

Name

Number the directions below each box to show how to make a pop-up card.

Draw a face, person, or animal on a third piece of paper. Color it and fold it in half with the picture side out.	Select two pieces of paper the same size.	Open the paper and push the cut strip though to the other side.	Apply glue on each side of the strip.
9	1	7	10
Fold the cut strip back and then fold it forward again.	Put your folded figure on the strip with glue. Decorate the rest of the inside.	Now glue the two papers together. Decorate the outside.	Start at the dots. Draw two parallel lines about 1 inch long toward the center of the front of the paper.
6	11	12	4
On one piece of paper, mark two dots about ½ inch apart in the middle of the folded edge.	Close the card and press firmly. Then open to see the pop-up strip.	Cut on the lines starting from the folded edge.	Fold each paper in half and then put one piece to the side.
3	8	5	2

Now follow the directions. If you have them in the right order you will be able to make a pop-up card.

• Circle the correct word to make the statement true.

A team wins a World Series (before, after) it wins the pennant.

Page 13

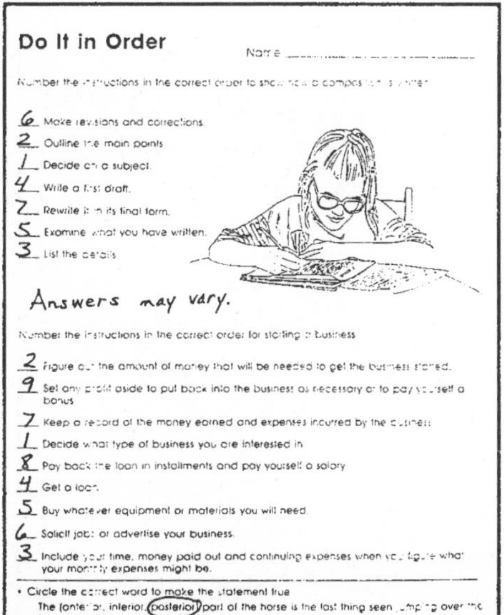

Do It in Order

Name

Number the instructions in the correct order to show how a composition is written.

6 Make revisions and corrections.
2 Outline the main points.
1 Decide on a subject.
4 Write a first draft.
7 Rewrite it in its final form.
5 Examine what you have written.
3 List the details.

Answers may vary.

Number the instructions in the correct order for starting a business.

2 Figure out the amount of money that will be needed to get the business started.
9 Set any profit aside to put back into the business as necessary or to pay yourself a bonus.
7 Keep a record of the money earned and expenses incurred by the business.
1 Decide what type of business you are interested in.
8 Pay back the loan in installments and pay yourself a salary.
4 Get a loan.
5 Buy whatever equipment or materials you will need.
6 Solicit jobs or advertise your business.
3 Include your time, money paid out and continuing expenses when you figure what your monthly expenses might be.

• Circle the correct word to make the statement true.

The (anterior, interior, posterior) part of the horse is the last thing seen jumping over the fence.

Page 14

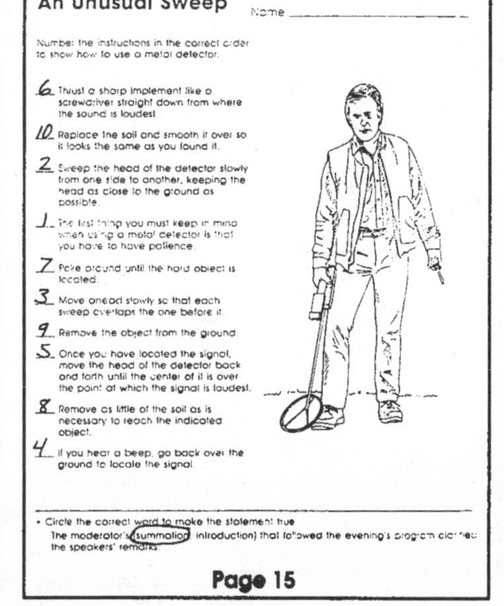

An Unusual Sweep

Name

Number the instructions in the correct order to show how to use a metal detector.

6 Thrust a sharp implement like a screwdriver straight down from where the sound is loudest.
10 Replace the soil and smooth it over so it looks the same as you found it.
2 Sweep the head of the detector slowly from one side to another, keeping the head as close to the ground as possible.
1 The first thing you must keep in mind when using a metal detector is that you have to have patience.
7 Poke around until the hard object is located.
3 Move ahead slowly so that each sweep overlaps the one before it.
9 Remove the object from the ground.
5 Once you have located the signal, move the head of the detector back and forth until the center of it is over the point at which the signal is loudest.
8 Remove as little of the soil as is necessary to reach the indicated object.
4 If you hear a beep, go back over the ground to locate the signal.

• Circle the correct word to make the statement true.

The moderator's (summation, introduction) that followed the evening's program clarified the speakers' remarks.

Page 15

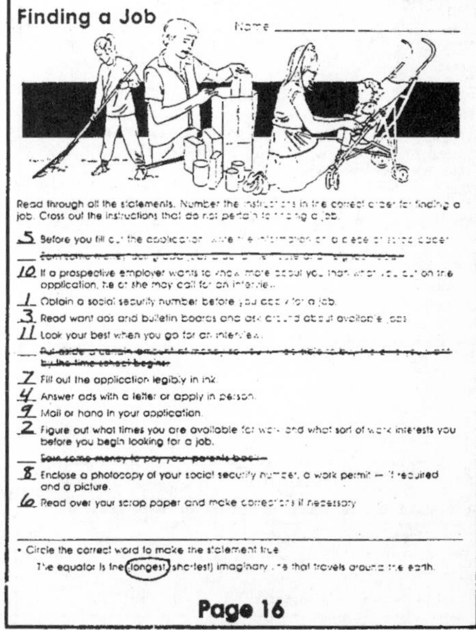

Finding a Job

Name

Read through all the statements. Number the instructions in the correct order for finding a job. Cross out the instructions that do not pertain to finding a job.

5 Before you fill out the application, write the information on a piece of scrap paper.
~~Sometime the [illegible]~~
10 If a prospective employer wants to know more about you than what you put on the application, he or she may call for an interview.
1 Obtain a social security number before you look for a job.
3 Read want ads and bulletin boards and ask around about available jobs.
11 Look your best when you go for an interview.
~~Put aside a certain amount of money [illegible] by the time school begins.~~
7 Fill out the application legibly in ink.
4 Answer ads with a letter or apply in person.
9 Mail or hand in your application.
2 Figure out what times you are available for work and what sort of work interests you before you begin looking for a job.
~~Earn some money to pay your parents back.~~
8 Enclose a photocopy of your social security number, a work permit — if required and a picture.
6 Read over your scrap paper and make corrections if necessary.

• Circle the correct word to make the statement true.

The equator is the (longest, shortest) imaginary line that travels around the earth.

Page 16

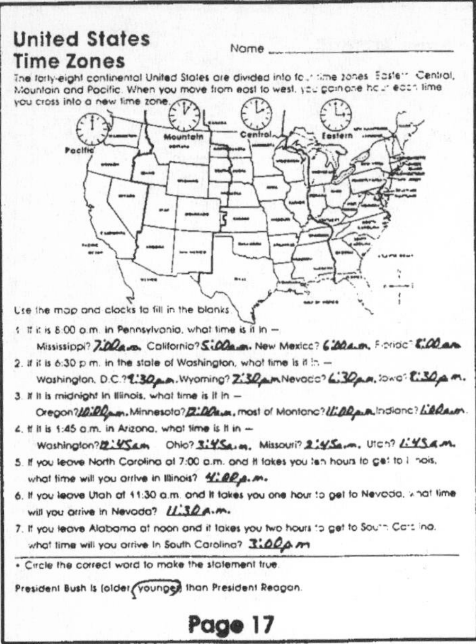

United States Time Zones

Name ____________

The forty-eight continental United States are divided into four time zones: Eastern, Central, Mountain and Pacific. When you move from east to west, you gain one hour each time you cross into a new time zone.

Use the map and clocks to fill in the blanks.

1. If it is 8:00 a.m. in Pennsylvania, what time is it in — Mississippi? 7:00 a.m. California? 5:00 a.m. New Mexico? 6:00 a.m. Florida? 8:00 a.m.
2. If it is 6:30 p.m. in the state of Washington, what time is it in — Washington, D.C.? 9:30 p.m. Wyoming? 7:30 p.m. Nevada? 6:30 p.m. Iowa? 8:30 p.m.
3. If it is midnight in Illinois, what time is it in — Oregon? 10:00 p.m. Minnesota? 12:00 a.m. most of Montana? 11:00 p.m. Indiana? 1:00 a.m.
4. If it is 1:45 a.m. in Arizona, what time is it in — Washington? 12:45 a.m. Ohio? 3:45 a.m. Missouri? 2:45 a.m. Utah? 1:45 a.m.
5. If you leave North Carolina at 7:00 a.m. and it takes you ten hours to get to Illinois, what time will you arrive in Illinois? 4:00 p.m.
6. If you leave Utah at 11:30 a.m. and it takes you one hour to get to Nevada, what time will you arrive in Nevada? 11:30 a.m.
7. If you leave Alabama at noon and it takes you two hours to get to South Carolina, what time will you arrive in South Carolina? 3:00 p.m.

• Circle the correct word to make the statement true.

President Bush is (older, **younger**) than President Reagan.

Page 17

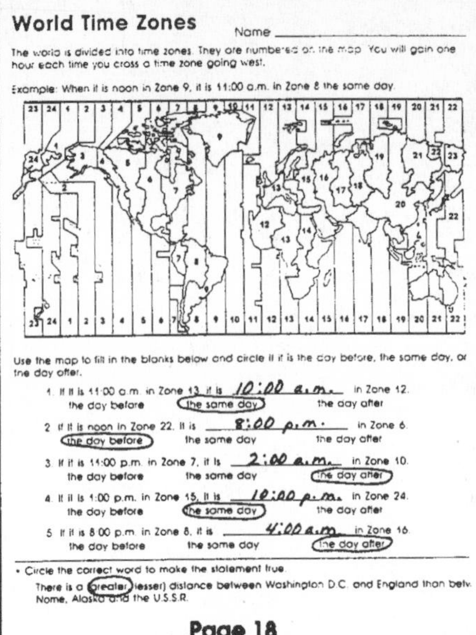

World Time Zones

Name ____________

The world is divided into time zones. They are numbered on the map. You will gain one hour each time you cross a time zone going west.

Example: When it is noon in Zone 9, it is 11:00 a.m. in Zone 8 the same day.

Use the map to fill in the blanks below and circle if it is the day before, the same day, or the day after.

1. If it is 11:00 a.m. in Zone 13, it is 10:00 a.m. in Zone 12. the day before / **the same day** / the day after
2. If it is noon in Zone 22, it is 8:00 p.m. in Zone 6. **the day before** / the same day / the day after
3. If it is 11:00 p.m. in Zone 7, it is 2:00 a.m. in Zone 10. the day before / the same day / **the day after**
4. If it is 1:00 p.m. in Zone 15, it is 10:00 p.m. in Zone 24. the day before / **the same day** / the day after
5. If it is 8:00 p.m. in Zone 8, it is 4:00 a.m. in Zone 16. the day before / the same day / **the day after**

• Circle the correct word to make the statement true.

There is a (**greater**, lesser) distance between Washington D.C. and England than between Nome, Alaska and the U.S.S.R.

Page 18

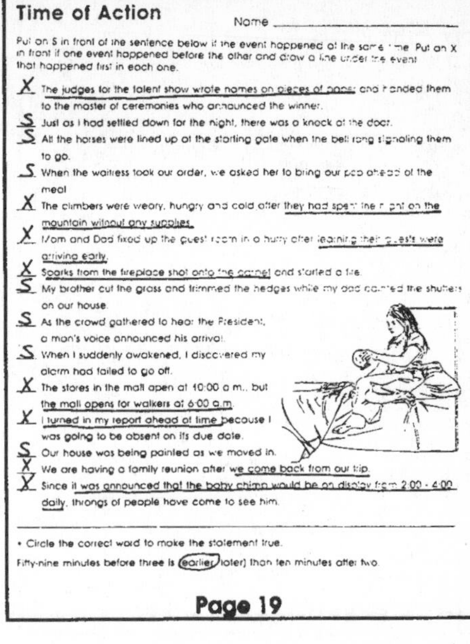

Time of Action

Name ____________

Put an S in front of the sentence below if the event happened at the same time. Put an X in front if one event happened before the other and draw a line under the event that happened first in each one.

X The judges for the talent show wrote names on pieces of paper and handed them to the master of ceremonies who announced the winner.
S Just as I had settled down for the night, there was a knock at the door.
S All the horses were lined up at the starting gate when the bell rang signaling them to go.
S When the waitress took our order, we asked her to bring our pop ahead of the meal.
X The climbers were weary, hungry and cold after they had spent the night on the mountain without any supplies.
X Mom and Dad fixed up the guest room in a hurry after learning their guests were arriving early.
X Sparks from the fireplace shot onto the carpet and started a fire.
S My brother cut the grass and trimmed the hedges while my dad painted the shutters on our house.
S As the crowd gathered to hear the President, a man's voice announced his arrival.
S When I suddenly awakened, I discovered my alarm had failed to go off.
X The stores in the mall open at 10:00 a.m., but the mall opens for walkers at 6:00 a.m.
X I turned in my report ahead of time because I was going to be absent on its due date.
S Our house was being painted as we moved in.
X We are having a family reunion after we come back from our trip.
X Since it was announced that the baby chimp would be on display from 2:00 - 4:00 daily, throngs of people have come to see him.

• Circle the correct word to make the statement true.

Fifty-nine minutes before three is (**earlier**, later) than ten minutes after two.

Page 19

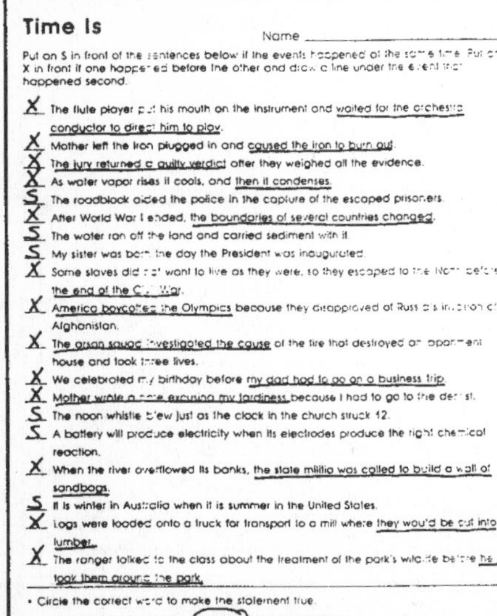

Time Is

Name ____________

Put an S in front of the sentences below if the events happened at the same time. Put an X in front if one happened before the other and draw a line under the event that happened second.

X The flute player put his mouth on the instrument and waited for the orchestra conductor to direct him to play.
X Mother left the iron plugged in and caused the iron to burn out.
X The jury returned a guilty verdict after they weighed all the evidence.
X As water vapor rises it cools, and then it condenses.
S The roadblock aided the police in the capture of the escaped prisoners.
X After World War I ended, the boundaries of several countries changed.
S The water ran off the land and carried sediment with it.
S My sister was born the day the President was inaugurated.
X Some slaves did not want to live as they were, so they escaped to the North before the end of the Civil War.
X America boycotted the Olympics because they disapproved of Russia's invasion of Afghanistan.
X The arson squad investigated the cause of the fire that destroyed an apartment house and took three lives.
X We celebrated my birthday before my dad had to go on a business trip.
X Mother wrote a note excusing my tardiness because I had to go to the dentist.
S The noon whistle blew just as the clock in the church struck 12.
S A battery will produce electricity when its electrodes produce the right chemical reaction.
X When the river overflowed its banks, the state militia was called to build a wall of sandbags.
S It is winter in Australia when it is summer in the United States.
X Logs were loaded onto a truck for transport to a mill where they would be cut into lumber.
X The ranger talked to the class about the treatment of the park's wildlife before he took them around the park.

• Circle the correct word to make the statement true.

An octogenarian is (older, **younger**) than a centenarian.

Page 20

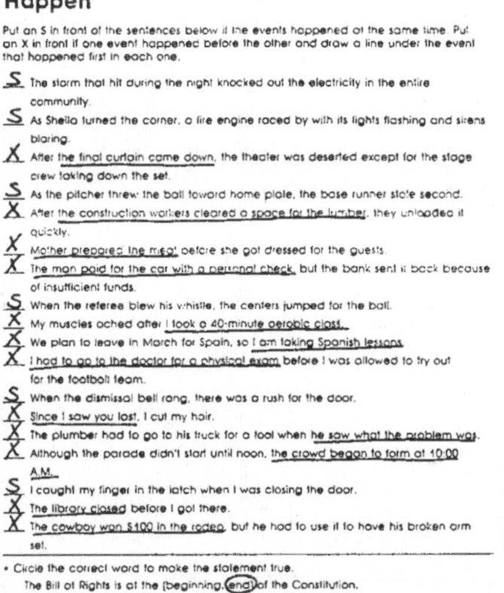

When Events Happen

Name ____________

Put an S in front of the sentences below if the events happened at the same time. Put an X in front if one event happened before the other and draw a line under the event that happened first in each one.

S The storm that hit during the night knocked out the electricity in the entire community.
S As Sheila turned the corner, a fire engine raced by with its lights flashing and sirens blaring.
X After the final curtain came down, the theater was deserted except for the stage crew taking down the set.
S As the pitcher threw the ball toward home plate, the base runner stole second.
X After the construction workers cleared a space for the lumber, they unloaded it quickly.
X Mother prepared the meal before she got dressed for the guests.
X The man paid for the car with a personal check, but the bank sent it back because of insufficient funds.
S When the referee blew his whistle, the centers jumped for the ball.
X My muscles ached after I took a 40-minute aerobic class.
X We plan to leave in March for Spain, so I am taking Spanish lessons.
X I had to go to the doctor for a physical exam before I was allowed to try out for the football team.
S When the dismissal bell rang, there was a rush for the door.
X Since I saw you last, I cut my hair.
X The plumber had to go to his truck for a tool when he saw what the problem was.
X Although the parade didn't start until noon, the crowd began to form at 10:00 A.M.
S I caught my finger in the latch when I was closing the door.
X The library closed before I got there.
X The cowboy won $100 in the rodeo, but he had to use it to have his broken arm set.

• Circle the correct word to make the statement true.

The Bill of Rights is at the (beginning, **end**) of the Constitution.

Page 21

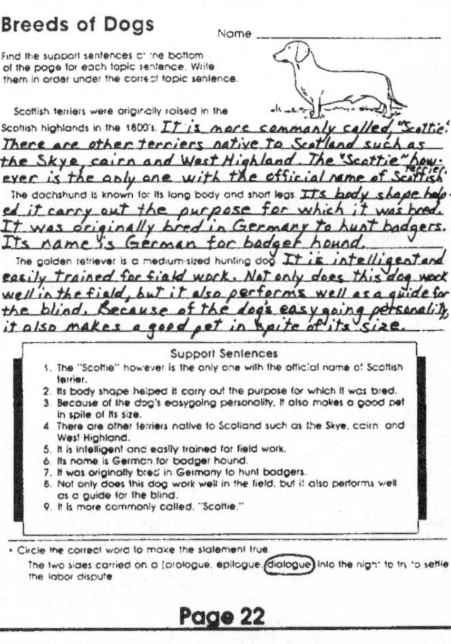

Breeds of Dogs

Name ____________

Find the support sentences at the bottom of the page for each topic sentence. Write them in order under the correct topic sentence.

Scottish terriers were originally raised in the Scottish highlands in the 1800's. It is more commonly called, "Scottie." There are other terriers native to Scotland such as the Skye, cairn and West Highland. The "Scottie" however is the only one with the official name of Scottish terrier.

The dachshund is known for its long body and short legs. Its body shape helped it carry out the purpose for which it was bred. It was originally bred in Germany to hunt badgers. Its name is German for badger hound.

The golden retriever is a medium-sized hunting dog. It is intelligent and easily trained for field work. Not only does this dog work well in the field, but it also performs well as a guide for the blind. Because of the dog's easygoing personality, it also makes a good pet in spite of its size.

Support Sentences

1. The "Scottie" however is the only one with the official name of Scottish terrier.
2. Its body shape helped it carry out the purpose for which it was bred.
3. Because of the dog's easygoing personality, it also makes a good pet in spite of its size.
4. There are other terriers native to Scotland such as the Skye, cairn and West Highland.
5. It is intelligent and easily trained for field work.
6. Its name is German for badger hound.
7. It was originally bred in Germany to hunt badgers.
8. Not only does this dog work well in the field, but it also performs well as a guide for the blind.
9. It is more commonly called, "Scottie."

• Circle the correct word to make the statement true.

The two sides carried on a (prologue, epilogue, **dialogue**) into the night to try to settle the labor dispute.

Page 22

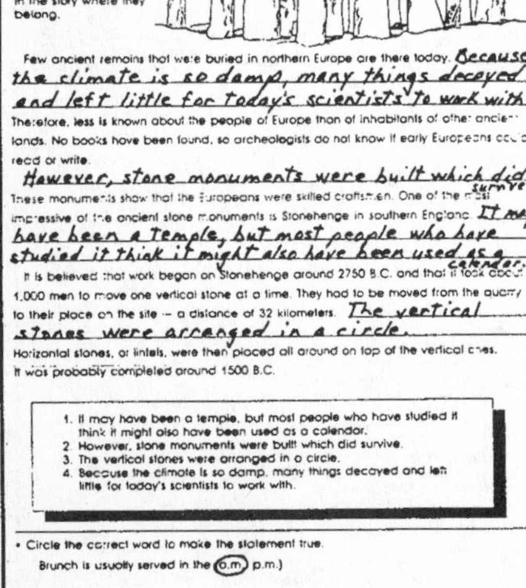

Stonehenge

Name ____________

The story is missing some of its sentences. Find them in the box below and write them in the story where they belong.

Few ancient remains that were buried in northern Europe are there today. Because the climate is so damp, many things decayed and left little for today's scientists to work with. Therefore, less is known about the people of Europe than of inhabitants of other ancient lands. No books have been found, so archeologists do not know if early Europeans could read or write. However, stone monuments were built which did survive. These monuments show that the Europeans were skilled craftsmen. One of the most impressive of the ancient stone monuments is Stonehenge in southern England. It may have been a temple, but most people who have studied it think it might also have been used as a calendar. It is believed that work began on Stonehenge around 2750 B.C. and that it took about 1,000 men to move one vertical stone at a time. They had to be moved from the quarry to their place on the site — a distance of 32 kilometers. The vertical stones were arranged in a circle. Horizontal stones, or lintels, were then placed all around on top of the vertical ones. It was probably completed around 1500 B.C.

1. It may have been a temple, but most people who have studied it think it might also have been used as a calendar.
2. However, stone monuments were built which did survive.
3. The vertical stones were arranged in a circle.
4. Because the climate is so damp, many things decayed and left little for today's scientists to work with.

• Circle the correct word to make the statement true.

Brunch is usually served in the (**a.m.**, p.m.)

Page 23

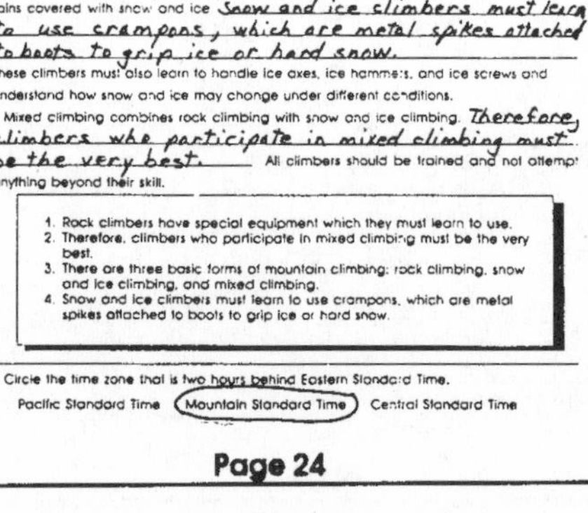

Forms of Mountain Climbing

Name ____________

The story is missing some of its sentences. Find them in the box below and write them in the story where they belong.

Mountain climbing is a sport that involves climbing mountains or just hiking in mountain country. There are three basic forms of mountain climbing: rock climbing, snow and ice climbing, and mixed climbing. Rock climbing involves climbing up rocky slopes. It is popular with beginning climbers because they can practice on cliffs that are not too difficult to climb. Rock climbers have special equipment which they must learn to use. Two such pieces are a piton and a snap link. A piton is an iron spike. It is hammered into rock cracks and has a ring at one end from which a rope can be secured. A snap link is a steel clip which attaches a rope to a climber or a piton.

Snow and ice climbers venture out in winter and summer, wherever there are mountains covered with snow and ice. Snow and ice climbers must learn to use crampons, which are metal spikes attached to boots to grip ice or hard snow. These climbers must also learn to handle ice axes, ice hammers, and ice screws and understand how snow and ice may change under different conditions.

Mixed climbing combines rock climbing with snow and ice climbing. Therefore, climbers who participate in mixed climbing must be the very best. All climbers should be trained and not attempt anything beyond their skill.

1. Rock climbers have special equipment which they must learn to use.
2. Therefore, climbers who participate in mixed climbing must be the very best.
3. There are three basic forms of mountain climbing: rock climbing, snow and ice climbing, and mixed climbing.
4. Snow and ice climbers must learn to use crampons, which are metal spikes attached to boots to grip ice or hard snow.

• Circle the time zone that is two hours behind Eastern Standard Time.

Pacific Standard Time (**Mountain Standard Time**) Central Standard Time

Page 24

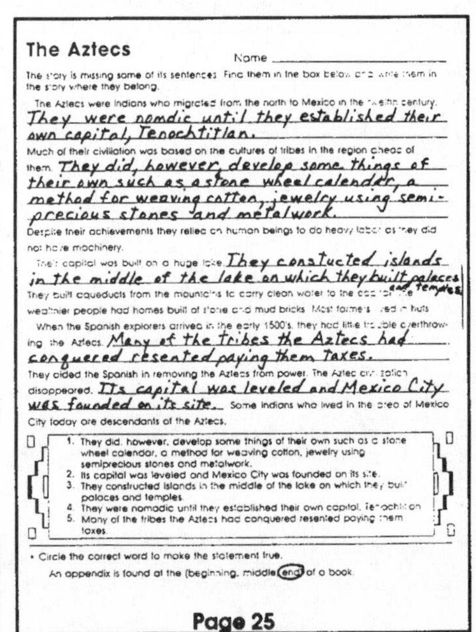

The Aztecs

Name ____________

The story is missing some of its sentences. Find them in the box below and write them in the story where they belong.

The Aztecs were Indians who migrated from the north to Mexico in the twelfth century. They were nomadic until they established their own capital, Tenochtitlan. Much of their civilization was based on the cultures of tribes in the region ahead of them. They did, however, develop some things of their own such as a stone wheel calendar, a method for weaving cotton, jewelry using semi-precious stones and metalwork. Despite their achievements they relied on human beings to do heavy labor as they did not have machinery.

Their capital was built on a huge lake. They constructed islands in the middle of the lake on which they built palaces and temples. They built aqueducts from the mountains to carry clean water to the capital. The wealthier people had homes built of stone and mud bricks. Most farmers lived in huts.

When the Spanish explorers arrived in the early 1500's, they had little trouble overthrowing the Aztecs. Many of the tribes the Aztecs had conquered resented paying them taxes. They aided the Spanish in removing the Aztecs from power. The Aztec civilization disappeared. Its capital was leveled and Mexico City was founded on its site. Some Indians who lived in the area of Mexico City today are descendants of the Aztecs.

1. They did, however, develop some things of their own such as a stone wheel calendar, a method for weaving cotton, jewelry using semiprecious stones and metalwork.
2. Its capital was leveled and Mexico City was founded on its site.
3. They constructed islands in the middle of the lake on which they built palaces and temples.
4. They were nomadic until they established their own capital, Tenochtitlan.
5. Many of the tribes the Aztecs had conquered resented paying them taxes.

• Circle the correct word to make the statement true.

An appendix is found at the (beginning, middle, **end**) of a book.

Page 25

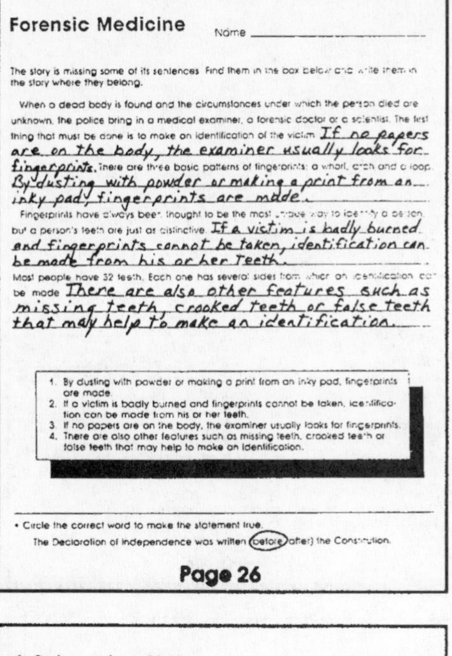

Forensic Medicine

Name ____________________

The story is missing some of its sentences. Find them in the box below and write them in the story where they belong.

When a dead body is found and the circumstances under which the person died are unknown, the police bring in a medical examiner, a forensic doctor or a scientist. The first thing that must be done is to make an identification of the victim. *If no papers are on the body, the examiner usually looks for fingerprints.* There are three basic patterns of fingerprints: a whorl, arch and a loop. *By dusting with powder or making a print from an inky pad, fingerprints are made.*

Fingerprints have always been thought to be the most unique way to identify a person, but a person's teeth are just as distinctive. *If a victim is badly burned and fingerprints cannot be taken, identification can be made from his or her teeth.* Most people have 32 teeth. Each one has several sides from which an identification can be made. *There are also other features such as missing teeth, crooked teeth or false teeth that may help to make an identification.*

1. By dusting with powder or making a print from an inky pad, fingerprints are made.
2. If a victim is badly burned and fingerprints cannot be taken, identification can be made from his or her teeth.
3. If no papers are on the body, the examiner usually looks for fingerprints.
4. There are also other features such as missing teeth, crooked teeth or false teeth that may help to make an identification.

• Circle the correct word to make the statement true.

The Declaration of Independence was written (**before**, after) the Constitution.

Page 26

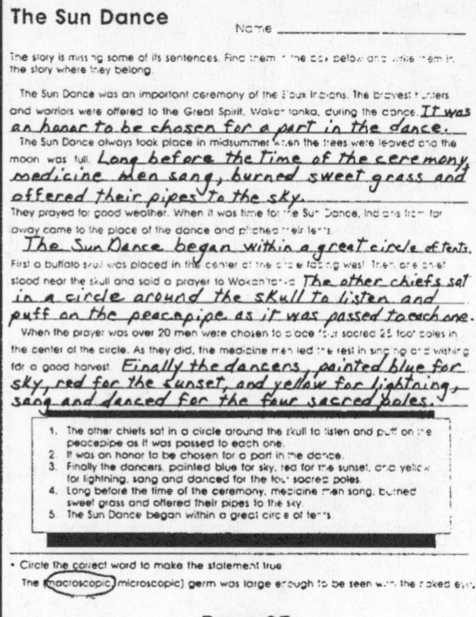

The Sun Dance

Name ____________________

The story is missing some of its sentences. Find them in the box below and write them in the story where they belong.

The Sun Dance was an important ceremony of the Sioux Indians. The bravest hunters and warriors were offered to the Great Spirit, Wakan tanka, during the dance. *It was an honor to be chosen for a part in the dance.*

The Sun Dance always took place in midsummer when the trees were leaved and the moon was full. *Long before the time of the ceremony, medicine men sang, burned sweet grass and offered their pipes to the sky.* They prayed for good weather. When it was time for the Sun Dance, Indians from far away came to the place of the dance and pitched their tents.

The Sun Dance began within a great circle of tents. First a buffalo skull was placed in the center of the circle facing west. Then one chief stood near the skull and said a prayer to Wakan tanka. *The other chiefs sat in a circle around the skull to listen and puff on the peacepipe as it was passed to each one.*

When the prayer was over 20 men were chosen to place four sacred 25 foot poles in the center of the circle. As they did, the medicine men led the rest in singing and wishing for a good harvest. *Finally the dancers, painted blue for sky, red for the sunset, and yellow for lightning, sang and danced for the four sacred poles.*

1. The other chiefs sat in a circle around the skull to listen and puff on the peacepipe as it was passed to each one.
2. It was an honor to be chosen for a part in the dance.
3. Finally the dancers, painted blue for sky, red for the sunset, and yellow for lightning, sang and danced for the four sacred poles.
4. Long before the time of the ceremony, medicine men sang, burned sweet grass and offered their pipes to the sky.
5. The Sun Dance began within a great circle of tents.

• Circle the correct word to make the statement true.

The (**macroscopic**, microscopic) germ was large enough to be seen with the naked eye.

Page 27

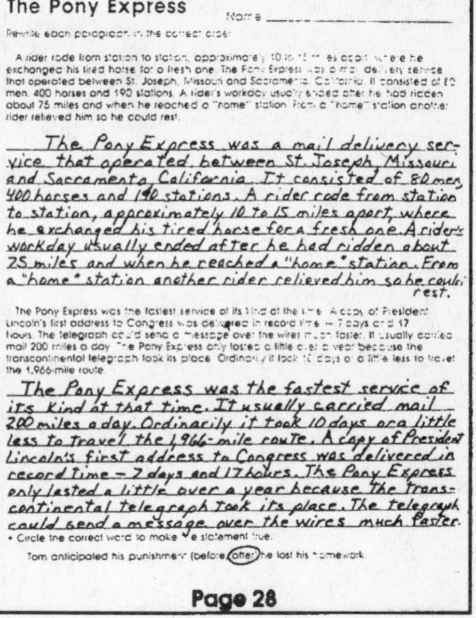

The Pony Express

Name ____________________

Rewrite each paragraph in the correct order.

A rider rode from station to station, approximately 10 to 15 miles apart, where he exchanged his tired horse for a fresh one. The Pony Express was a mail delivery service that operated between St. Joseph, Missouri and Sacramento, California. It consisted of 80 men, 400 horses and 190 stations. A rider's workday usually ended after he had ridden about 75 miles and when he reached a "home" station. From a "home" station another rider relieved him so he could rest.

The Pony Express was a mail delivery service that operated between St. Joseph, Missouri and Sacramento, California. It consisted of 80 men, 400 horses and 190 stations. A rider rode from station to station, approximately 10 to 15 miles apart, where he exchanged his tired horse for a fresh one. A rider's workday usually ended after he had ridden about 75 miles and when he reached a "home" station. From a "home" station another rider relieved him so he could rest.

The Pony Express was the fastest service of its kind at the time. A copy of President Lincoln's first address to Congress was delivered in record time — 7 days and 17 hours. The telegraph could send a message over the wires much faster. It usually carried mail 200 miles a day. The Pony Express only lasted a little over a year because the transcontinental telegraph took its place. Ordinarily it took 10 days or a little less to travel the 1,966-mile route.

The Pony Express was the fastest service of its kind at that time. It usually carried mail 200 miles a day. Ordinarily it took 10 days or a little less to travel the 1,966-mile route. A copy of President Lincoln's first address to Congress was delivered in record time — 7 days and 17 hours. The Pony Express only lasted a little over a year because the transcontinental telegraph took its place. The telegraph could send a message over the wires much faster.

• Circle the correct word to make the statement true.

Tom anticipated his punishment (before, **after**) he lost his homework.

Page 28

A Submarine Strikes

Name ____________________

Rewrite each paragraph about a United States Naval battle in a sensible order.

They were the battleships that had fought the United States Navy a few days before. A periscope suddenly popped up through the water in the Pacific Ocean. The captain ordered the crew to be ready for battle. It turned from one side to the other. There were four ships sailing along. It focused on something and stopped.

A periscope suddenly popped up through the water in the Pacific Ocean. It turned from one side to the other. It focused on something and stopped. There were four ships sailing along. They were the battleships that had fought the United States Navy a few days before. The captain ordered the crew to be ready for battle.

As the last ship passed, he gave the order to fire. The captain of the U.S. submarine kept an eye on the ships as they passed about ½ mile away. The crew sent four torpedoes toward the enemy ship. No one saw the other torpedoes strike, but they could feel the explosions as they submerged. The captain saw the first torpedo hit. Then the captain shouted, "Dive!" and the sub went under. It hit with such force that the crew on the sub felt the shock.

The captain of the U.S. submarine kept an eye on the ships as they passed about ½ mile away. As the last ship passed, he gave the order to fire. The crew sent four torpedoes toward the enemy ship. The captain saw the first torpedo hit. It hit with such force that the crew on the sub felt the shock. Then the captain shouted, "Dive!" and the sub went under. No one saw the other torpedoes strike, but they could feel the explosions as they submerged.

• Circle the correct word to make the statement true.

The preface is at the (**beginning**, middle, end) of a book.

Page 29

Sea Sagas

Name ____________________

Rewrite each paragraph about a shipwreck in a sensible order.

The ship has been sighted several times drifting without a crew, but it has never been captured. One sea tale tells of a ship trapped by ice off the coast of Alaska during a storm. Could that ghost ship still be sailing in the Arctic seas? When the storm ended the ship was gone. The crew, fearing the ship would be crushed to pieces by the ice, abandoned ship and pitched tents on a nearby beach.

One sea tale tells of a ship trapped by ice off the coast of Alaska during a storm. The crew, fearing the ship would be crushed to pieces by the ice, abandoned ship and pitched tents on a nearby beach. When the storm ended the ship was gone. The ship has been sighted several times drifting without a crew, but it has never been captured. Could that ghost ship still be sailing in the Arctic seas?

In 1861 the Maritana was wrecked and most of its crew were killed. Some thought that the spirit of a ship lived in its figurehead and would protect the crew from danger. Sailors held several superstitions about the sea. It was the third time a ship bearing that same figurehead sank, but the figurehead remained unharmed. On the other hand, some figureheads were considered unlucky.

Sailors held several superstitions about the sea. Some thought that the spirit of a ship lived in its figurehead and would protect the crew from danger. On the other hand, some figureheads were considered unlucky. In 1861 the Maritana was wrecked and most of its crew were killed. It was the third time a ship bearing that same figurehead sank, but the figurehead remained unharmed.

• Circle the correct word to make the statement true.

A/An (antecedent, **precedent**) is set before the fact.

Page 30

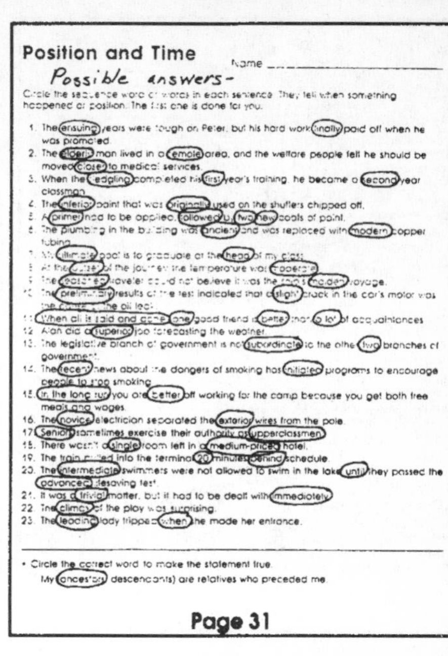

Position and Time

Name ____________________

Possible answers-

Circle the sequence word or words in each sentence. They tell when something happened or position. The first one is done for you.

1. The **ensuing** years were tough on Peter, but his hard work **finally** paid off when he was promoted.
2. The **elderly** man lived in a **remote** area, and the welfare people felt he should be moved **closer** to medical services.
3. When the **fledgling** completed his **first** year's training, he became a **second** year classman.
4. The **inferior** paint that was **originally** used on the shutters chipped off.
5. A **primer** had to be applied, **followed by two new** coats of paint.
6. The plumbing in the building was **ancient** and was replaced with **modern** copper tubing.
7. My **ultimate** goal is to graduate at the **head** of my class.
8. At the **outset** of the journey the temperature was **moderate**.
9. The **seasoned** traveler could not believe it was the ship's **maiden** voyage.
10. The **preliminary** results of the test indicated that a **slight** crack in the car's motor was the cause of the oil leak.
11. **When all is said and done**, **one** good friend is **better** than **a lot** of acquaintances.
12. Alan did a **superior** job forecasting the weather.
13. The legislative branch of government is not **subordinate** to the other **two** branches of government.
14. The **recent** news about the dangers of smoking has **initiated** programs to encourage people to stop smoking.
15. **In the long run** you are **better** off working for the camp because you get both free meals and wages.
16. The **novice** electrician separated the **exterior** wires from the pole.
17. **Seniors** sometimes exercise their authority as **upperclassmen**.
18. There wasn't a **single** room left in a **medium-priced** hotel.
19. The train pulled into the terminal **20** minutes **behind** schedule.
20. The **intermediate** swimmers were not allowed to swim in the lake **until** they passed the **advanced** lifesaving test.
21. It was a **trivial** matter, but it had to be dealt with **immediately**.
22. The **climax** of the play was surprising.
23. The **leading** lady tripped **when** she made her entrance.

• Circle the correct word to make the statement true.

My (**ancestors**, descendants) are relatives who preceded me.

Page 31

So What Now?

Name ____________________

Match the two sentence parts. Write the number of the first part on the line in front of its last part.

1. If you eat food that's good for you
2. If the strange dog bites you
3. If the typewriter breaks down
4. If the fabric begins to fray
5. If the tennis game is canceled
6. If you put the red shirt in with the white sheets
7. If debts are paid promptly
8. If a horse breaks its leg
9. If you brush your teeth after every meal
10. If Mrs. Jones calls for me
11. If there is a storm from the east
12. If there is a heavy snowfall during the winter
13. If the book isn't on the shelf
14. If you have a bug bite
15. If you get the wrong number
16. If there is an electrical storm
17. If there are no objections
18. If there is a fire in a skyscraper
19. If a person is injured
20. If the only lights that go out are in the kitchen
21. If I can't keep the hair out of my eyes
22. If a dollar is worth 100 pennies
23. If you pay in advance for your theater seats

4 sew it around the edge.
9 it should help cut down on your dentistry bills.
14 it's best not to scratch it.
20 check the circuit breakers.
2 you must report it to the rabies control.
12 its runoff may cause rivers to overflow.
18 do not use the elevator.
21 I'm going to tie it back.
6 your bedclothes will turn pink.
11 the rain will seep through our east window.
16 it's best not to talk on the telephone.
7 a person establishes good credit.
13 ask the librarian if it is checked out.
10 tell her I will return soon.
15 dial information.
1 you will be healthier.
19 it is best not to move him until medical help arrives.
23 there is a fifteen percent reduction.
8 it usually is destroyed.
22 five dollars equal 500 pennies.
3 you will have to write the report by hand.
17 we will continue.
5 I will have to reschedule it.

• Circle the correct word to make the statement true.

The (primitive, **extinct**) bird can no longer be found anywhere on Earth.

Page 32

You Did It

Name ____________________

Write each cause on the line before or after its effect. Each cause will be used only once.

Causes

- two of their fellow workers had been fired unnecessarily
- his mother had seen a small creature in her pantry
- they won the state championship.
- Since we moved our clocks ahead,
- to use to build their winter nests.
- there was an unusual amount of rain.
- he received the call on his car radio.
- to avoid hitting the small boy.
- Very little light reached the forest floor through the thick foliage.
- After we finished all our work,
- the class performed a smelly science experiment.
- I go to an aerobic class after work
- a fire gutted our home.
- they did not like the school's menu.

1. The ball team was given a grand welcome at the airport after *they won the state championship.*
2. The driver swerved his car into a tree *to avoid hitting the small boy.*
3. Our flowers blossomed early this year because *there was an unusual amount of rain.*
4. The teacher opened all the windows after *the class performed a smelly science experiment.*
5. The factory workmen were striking because *two of their fellow workers had been fired unnecessarily.*
6. *Very little light reached the forest floor through the thick foliage,* so it was dark and damp.
7. Squirrels ran from tree to tree gathering twigs *to use to build their winter nests.*
8. *I go to an aerobic class after work* because it gives me more energy.
9. *Since we moved our clocks ahead,* it stays light out later.
10. We bought new furniture after *a fire gutted our home.*
11. Most of the class brought their lunch because *they did not like the school's menu.*
12. The police officer arrived within minutes after *he received the call on his car radio.*
13. Teddy set a trap because *his mother had seen a small creature in her pantry.*
14. *After we finished all our work,* father treated us to ice cream.

• Circle the correct word to make the statement true.

A (**decathlon**, heptathlon) has ten athletic events.

Page 33

Now What?

Name ____________________

Each sentence is either missing a cause or an effect. Find it in the box and add it to the sentence. Next write C in front of each sentence to which you added a cause or E in front of each one to which an effect was added.

- [C] *When the light is yellow,* a driver should prepare to stop.
- [E] The August sun was so blistering hot *that the grass turned as yellow as straw.*
- [E] When mother cut herself in the kitchen, *I applied a tourniquet and drove her to the hospital.*
- [C] *There was nothing good on television, so* we went to the movies.
- [E] When the bell rang at the end of the first period, *I went to my second-hour class.*
- [C] *Every time the stock market goes down,* my father gets upset.
- [E] When juniper is in bloom, *my allergies are very active.*
- [C] *The telephone rang and* I answered it.
- [E] When I opened the door to let the dog in, *the wind blew the lamp over.*
- [E] I didn't sleep last night and *I'm tired today.*
- [E] The boy broke his arm when he fell from the tree and *the doctor put it in a cast.*
- [E] It was so cold out that *our pipes froze.*

my allergies are very active
the wind blew the lamp over.
When the light is yellow,
Every time the stock market goes down,
The telephone rang and
I went to my second-hour class.
the doctor put it in a cast.
I applied a tourniquet and drove her to the hospital.
our pipes froze.
I'm tired today.
that the grass turned as yellow as straw.
There was nothing good on television, so

• Circle the correct word to make the statement true.

The man had a premonition that something would go wrong (after, **before**) it happen-

Page 34

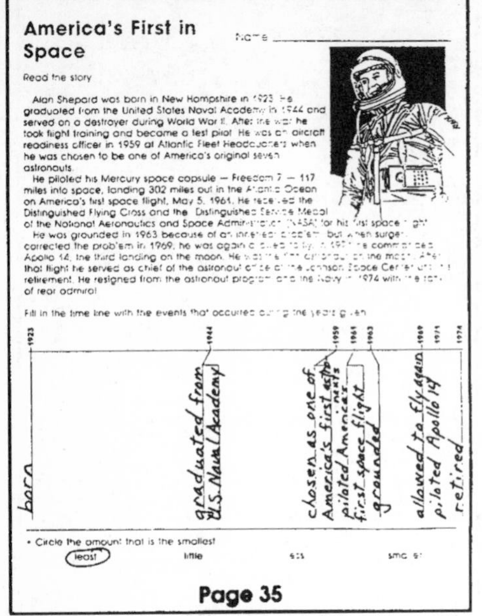

America's First in Space

Name

Read the story.

Alan Shepard was born in New Hampshire in 1923. He graduated from the United States Naval Academy in 1944 and served on a destroyer during World War II. After the war he took flight training and became a test pilot. He was an aircraft readiness officer in 1959 at Atlantic Fleet Headquarters when he was chosen to be one of America's original seven astronauts.

He piloted his Mercury space capsule — Freedom 7 — 117 miles into space, landing 302 miles out in the Atlantic Ocean on America's first space flight, May 5, 1961. He received the Distinguished Flying Cross and the Distinguished Service Medal of the National Aeronautics and Space Administration (NASA) for his first space flight.

He was grounded in 1963 because of an inner-ear problem, but when surgery corrected the problem in 1969, he was again allowed to fly. In 1971 he commanded Apollo 14, the third landing on the moon. He was the fifth astronaut on the moon. After that flight he served as chief of the astronaut office at the Johnson Space Center until his retirement. He resigned from the astronaut program and the Navy in 1974 with the rank of rear admiral.

Fill in the time line with the events that occurred during the years given.

1923 — born
1944 — graduated from U.S. Naval Academy
1959 — chosen as one of America's first astronauts
1961 — piloted America's first space flight
1963 — grounded
1969 — allowed to fly again
1971 — piloted Apollo 14
1974 — retired

• Circle the amount that is the smallest.
(least) little less small

Page 35

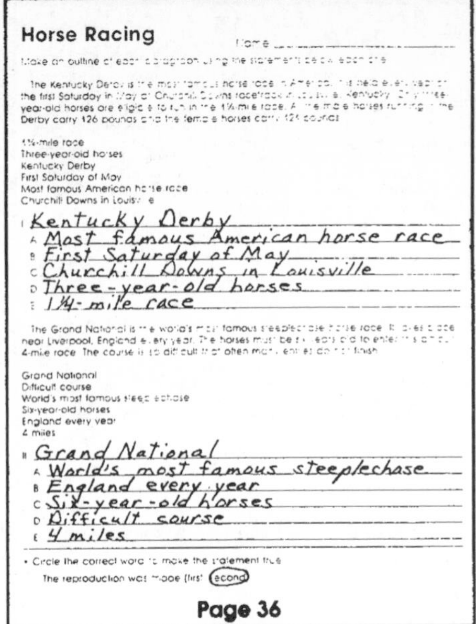

Horse Racing

Name

Make an outline of each paragraph using the statements below each one.

The Kentucky Derby is the most famous horse race in America. It is held every year on the first Saturday in May at Churchill Downs racetrack in Louisville, Kentucky. Only three-year-old horses are eligible to run in the 1¼-mile race. All the male horses running in the Derby carry 126 pounds and the female horses carry 121 pounds.

1¼-mile race
Three-year-old horses
Kentucky Derby
First Saturday of May
Most famous American horse race
Churchill Downs in Louisville

I. Kentucky Derby
A. Most famous American horse race
B. First Saturday of May
C. Churchill Downs in Louisville
D. Three-year-old horses
E. 1¼-mile race

The Grand National is the world's most famous steeplechase horse race. It takes place near Liverpool, England every year. The horses must be six years old to enter this difficult 4-mile race. The course is so difficult that often many entries do not finish.

Grand National
Difficult course
World's most famous steeplechase
Six-year-old horses
England every year
4 miles

II. Grand National
A. World's most famous steeplechase
B. England every year
C. Six-year-old horses
D. Difficult course
E. 4 miles

• Circle the correct word to make the statement true.
The reproduction was made (first, (second)).

Page 36

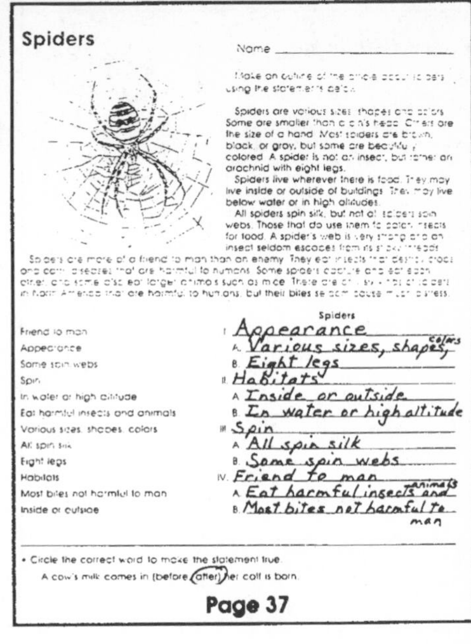

Spiders

Name

Make an outline of the article about spiders using the statements below.

Spiders are various sizes, shapes and colors. Some are smaller than a pin's head. Others are the size of a hand. Most spiders are brown, black, or gray, but some are beautifully colored. A spider is not an insect, but rather an arachnid with eight legs.

Spiders live wherever there is food. They may live inside or outside of buildings. They may live below water or in high altitudes.

All spiders spin silk, but not all spiders spin webs. Those that do use them to catch insects for food. A spider's web is very strong and an insect seldom escapes from its sticky threads.

Spiders are more of a friend to man than an enemy. They eat insects that destroy crops and carry diseases that are harmful to humans. Some spiders capture and eat each other, and some also eat larger animals such as mice. There are only a few spiders in North America that are harmful to humans, but their bites seldom cause much distress.

Friend to man
Appearance
Some spin webs
Spin
In water or high altitude
Eat harmful insects and animals
Various sizes, shapes, colors
All spin silk
Eight legs
Habitats
Most bites not harmful to man
Inside or outside

Spiders
I. Appearance
A. Various sizes, shapes, colors
B. Eight legs
II. Habitats
A. Inside or outside
B. In water or high altitude
III. Spin
A. All spin silk
B. Some spin webs
IV. Friend to man
A. Eat harmful insects and animals
B. Most bites not harmful to man

• Circle the correct word to make the statement true.
A cow's milk comes in (before, (after)) her calf is born.

Page 37

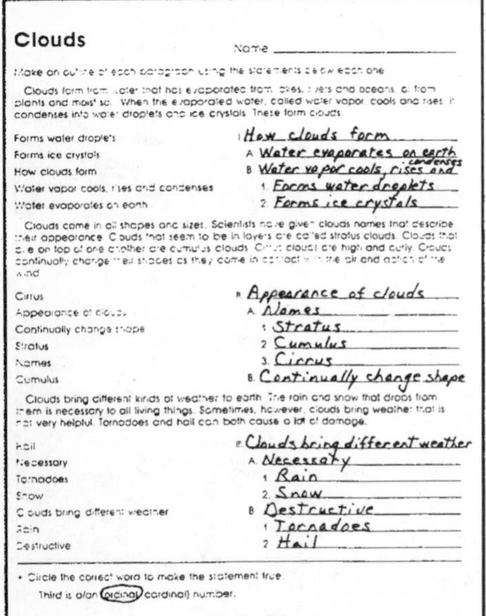

Clouds

Name

Make an outline of each paragraph using the statements below each one.

Clouds form from water that has evaporated from lakes, rivers and oceans, or from plants and moist soil. When the evaporated water, called water vapor, cools and rises, it condenses into water droplets and ice crystals. These form clouds.

Forms water droplets
Forms ice crystals
How clouds form
Water vapor cools, rises and condenses
Water evaporates on earth

I. How clouds form
A. Water evaporates on earth
B. Water vapor cools, rises and condenses
1. Forms water droplets
2. Forms ice crystals

Clouds come in all shapes and sizes. Scientists have given clouds names that describe their appearance. Clouds that seem to be in layers are called stratus clouds. Clouds that are on top of one another are cumulus clouds. Cirrus clouds are high and curly. Clouds continually change their shapes as they come in contact with the air and action of the wind.

Cirrus
Appearance of clouds
Continually change shape
Stratus
Names
Cumulus

II. Appearance of clouds
A. Names
1. Stratus
2. Cumulus
3. Cirrus
B. Continually change shape

Clouds bring different kinds of weather to earth. The rain and snow that drops from them is necessary to all living things. Sometimes, however, clouds bring weather that is not very helpful. Tornadoes and hail can both cause a lot of damage.

Hail
Necessary
Tornadoes
Snow
Clouds bring different weather
Rain
Destructive

III. Clouds bring different weather
A. Necessary
1. Rain
2. Snow
B. Destructive
1. Tornadoes
2. Hail

• Circle the correct word to make the statement true.
Third is a(n) ((ordinal), cardinal) number.

Page 38

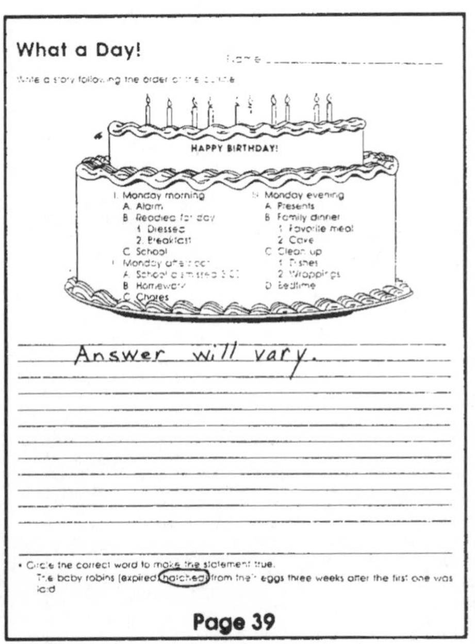

What a Day!

Name

Write a story following the order of the outline.

Answer will vary.

• Circle the correct word to make the statement true.
The baby robins (expired, (hatched)) from their eggs three weeks after the first one was laid.

Page 39

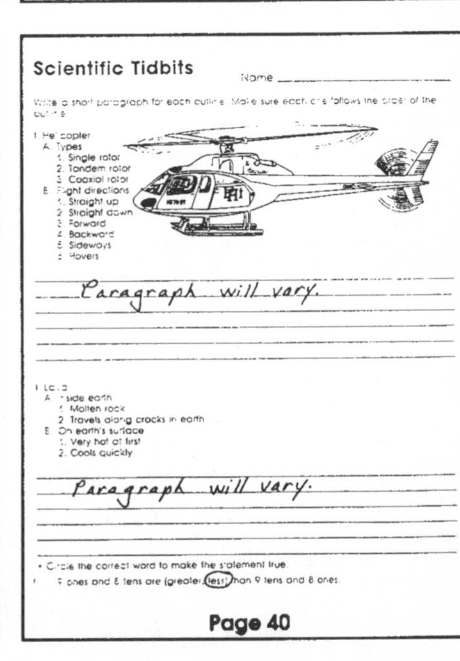

Scientific Tidbits

Name

Write a short paragraph for each outline. Make sure each one follows the order of the outline.

I. Helicopter
A. Types
1. Single rotor
2. Tandem rotor
3. Coaxial rotor
B. Flight directions
1. Straight up
2. Straight down
3. Forward
4. Backward
5. Sideways
6. Hovers

Paragraph will vary.

II. Lava
A. Inside earth
1. Molten rock
2. Travels along cracks in earth
B. On earth's surface
1. Very hot at first
2. Cools quickly

Paragraph will vary.

• Circle the correct word to make the statement true.
7 ones and 8 tens are (greater, (less)) than 9 tens and 8 ones.

Page 40

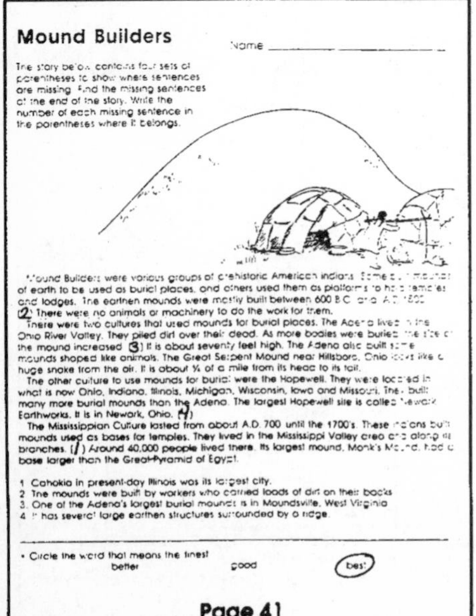

Mound Builders

Name

The story below contains four sets of parentheses to show where sentences are missing. Find the missing sentences at the end of the story. Write the number of each missing sentence in the parentheses where it belongs.

Mound Builders were various groups of prehistoric American Indians. Some built mounds of earth to be used as burial places, and others used them as platforms to hold temples and lodges. The earthen mounds were mostly built between 600 B.C. and A.D. 1600. (2) There were no animals or machinery to do the work for them.

There were two cultures that used mounds for burial places. The Adena lived in the Ohio River Valley. They piled dirt over their dead. As more bodies were buried, the size of the mound increased. (3) It is about seventy feet high. The Adena also built some mounds shaped like animals. The Great Serpent Mound near Hillsboro, Ohio looks like a huge snake from the air. It is about ¼ of a mile from its head to its tail.

The other culture to use mounds for burial were the Hopewell. They were located in what is now Ohio, Indiana, Illinois, Michigan, Wisconsin, Iowa and Missouri. They built many more burial mounds than the Adena. The largest Hopewell site is called Newark Earthworks. It is in Newark, Ohio. (4)

The Mississippian Culture lasted from about A.D. 700 until the 1700's. These Indians built mounds used as bases for temples. They lived in the Mississippi Valley area and along its branches. (1) Around 40,000 people lived there. Its largest mound, Monk's Mound, had a base larger than the Great Pyramid of Egypt.

1. Cahokia in present-day Illinois was its largest city.
2. The mounds were built by workers who carried loads of dirt on their backs.
3. One of the Adena's largest burial mounds is in Moundsville, West Virginia.
4. It has several large earthen structures surrounded by a ridge.

• Circle the word that means the finest.
better good (best)

Page 41

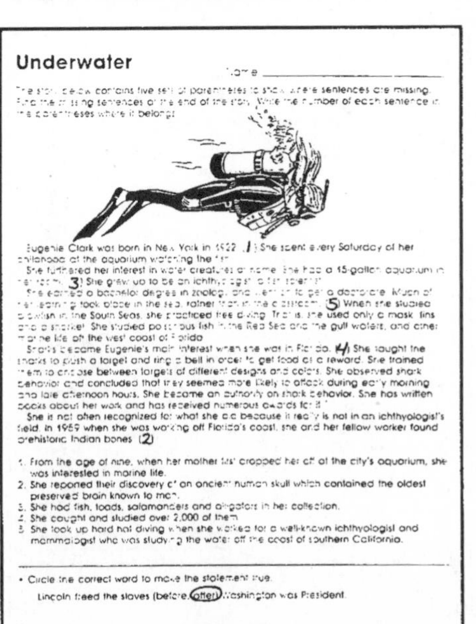

Underwater

Name

The story below contains five sets of parentheses to show where sentences are missing. Find the missing sentences at the end of the story. Write the number of each sentence in the parentheses where it belongs.

Eugenie Clark was born in New York in 1922. (1) She spent every Saturday of her childhood at the aquarium watching the fish.

She furthered her interest in water creatures at home. She had a 15-gallon aquarium in her room. (3) She grew up to be an ichthyologist or fish scientist.

She earned a bachelor degree in zoology and went on to get a doctorate. Much of her learning took place in the sea, rather than in the classroom. (5) When she studied fish in the South Seas, she practiced free diving. That is, she used only a mask, fins and a snorkel. She studied poisonous fish in the Red Sea and the gulf waters, and other marine life off the west coast of Florida.

Sharks became Eugenie's main interest when she was in Florida. (4) She taught the sharks to push a target and ring a bell in order to get food as a reward. She trained them to choose between targets of different designs and colors. She observed shark behavior and concluded that they seemed more likely to attack during early morning and late afternoon hours. She became an authority on shark behavior. She has written books about her work and has received numerous awards for it.

She is not often recognized for what she did because it really is not in an ichthyologist's field. In 1959 when she was working off Florida's coast, she and her fellow worker found prehistoric Indian bones. (2)

1. From the age of nine, when her mother first dropped her off at the city's aquarium, she was interested in marine life.
2. She reported their discovery of an ancient human skull which contained the oldest preserved brain known to man.
3. She had fish, toads, salamanders and alligators in her collection.
4. She caught and studied over 2,000 of them.
5. She took up hard hat diving when she worked for a well-known ichthyologist and mammalogist who was studying the water off the coast of southern California.

• Circle the correct word to make the statement true.
Lincoln freed the slaves (before, (after)) Washington was President.

Page 42

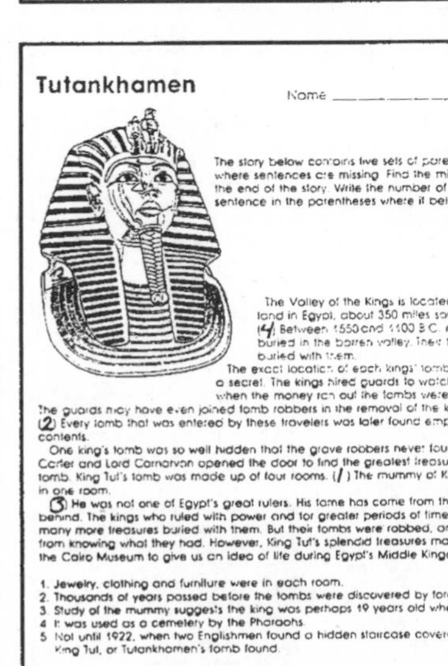

Tutankhamen

Name

The story below contains five sets of parentheses to show where sentences are missing. Find the missing sentences at the end of the story. Write the number of each missing sentence in the parentheses where it belongs.

The Valley of the Kings is located on barren desert land in Egypt, about 350 miles south of Cairo. (4) Between 1550 and 1100 B.C. many kings were buried in the barren valley. Their treasures were buried with them.

The exact location of each kings' tomb was meant to be a secret. The kings hired guards to watch the tombs, but when the money ran out the tombs were left unguarded. The guards may have even joined tomb robbers in the removal of the king's treasures. (2) Every tomb that was entered by these travelers was later found emptied of its contents.

One king's tomb was so well hidden that the grave robbers never found it. (5) Howard Carter and Lord Carnarvon opened the door to find the greatest treasure ever found in a tomb. King Tut's tomb was made up of four rooms. (1) The mummy of King Tut was found in one room.

(3) He was not one of Egypt's great rulers. His fame has come from the treasures he left behind. The kings who ruled with power and for greater periods of time probably had many more treasures buried with them. But their tombs were robbed, and so were we — from knowing what they had. However, King Tut's splendid treasures may be viewed in the Cairo Museum to give us an idea of life during Egypt's Middle Kingdom.

1. Jewelry, clothing and furniture were in each room.
2. Thousands of years passed before the tombs were discovered by foreign travelers.
3. Study of the mummy suggests the king was perhaps 19 years old when he died.
4. It was used as a cemetery by the Pharaohs.
5. Not until 1922, when two Englishmen found a hidden staircase covered by debris, was King Tut, or Tutankhamen's tomb found.

• Circle the correct word to make the statement true.
An average is the (top, (middle), bottom) figure.

Page 43